BEAUTIFUL PIANO SOLOS

You've Always Wanted To Play

ISBN 978-1-4234-9978-7

EXCLUSIVELY DISTRIBUTED BY

HAL•LEONARD®
CORPORATION
7777 W. BLUEMOUND RD. P.O. BOX 13819 MILWAUKEE, WI 53213

Visit Hal Leonard Online at
www.halleonard.com

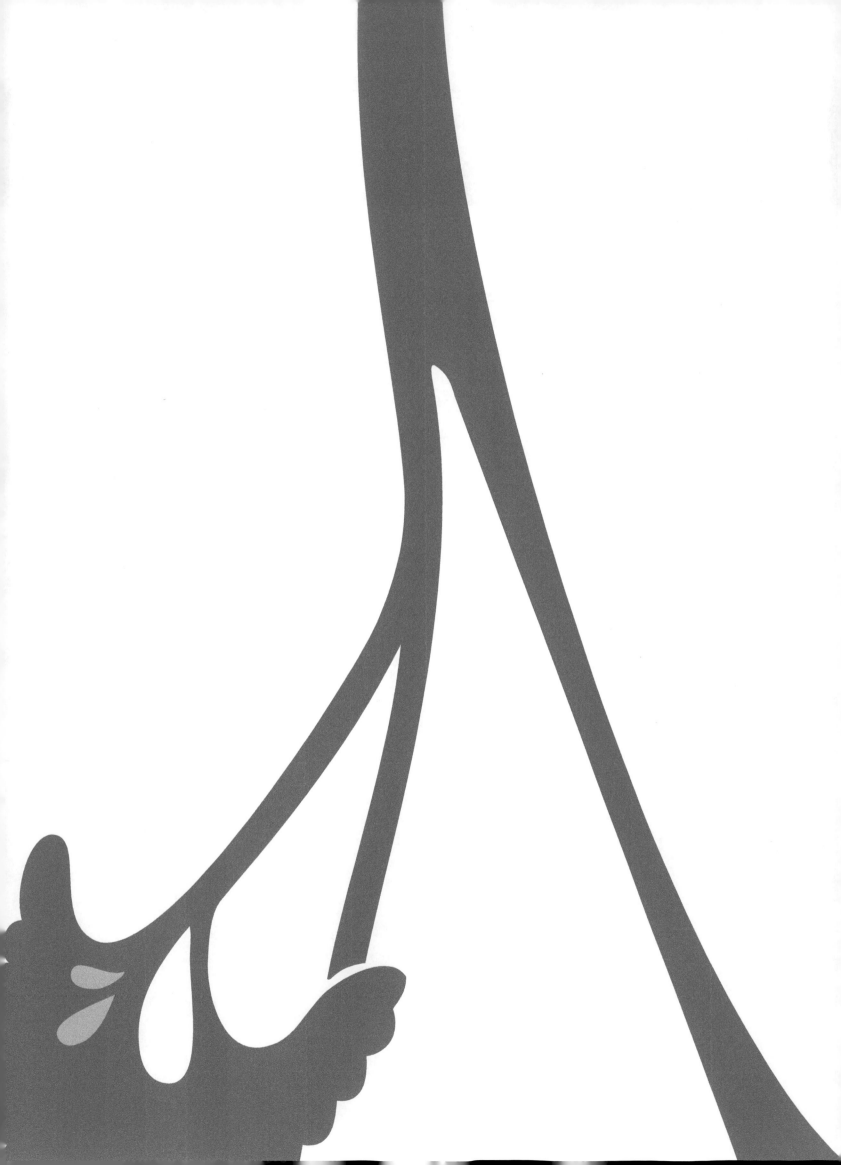

ALL THE THINGS YOU ARE

from VERY WARM FOR MAY

Lyrics by OSCAR HAMMERSTEIN II
Music by JEROME KERN

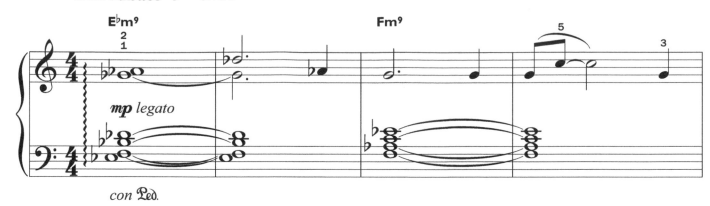

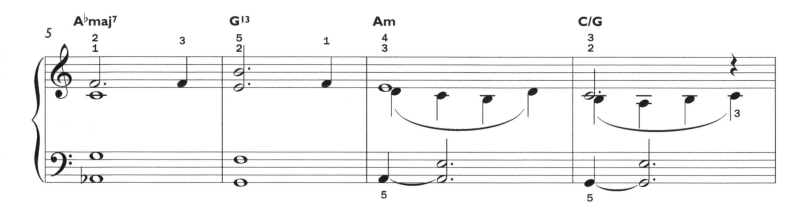

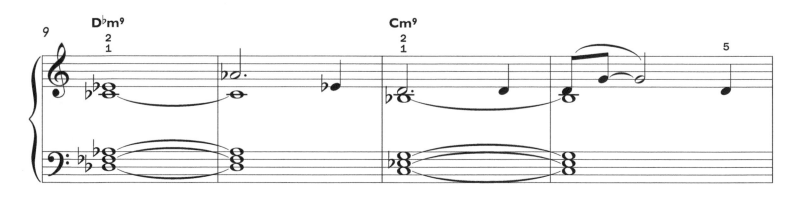

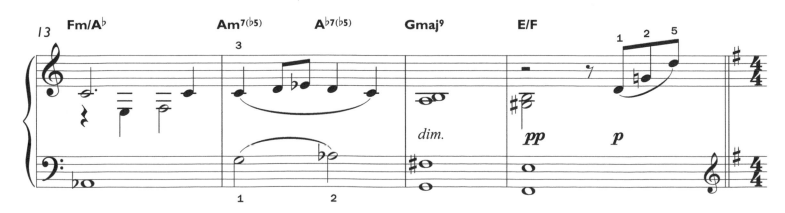

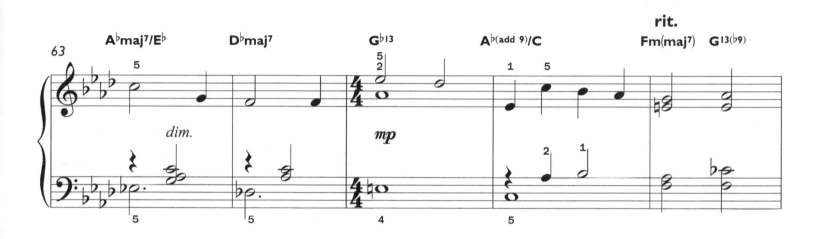

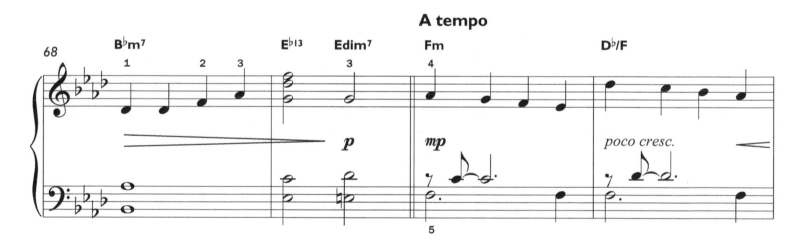

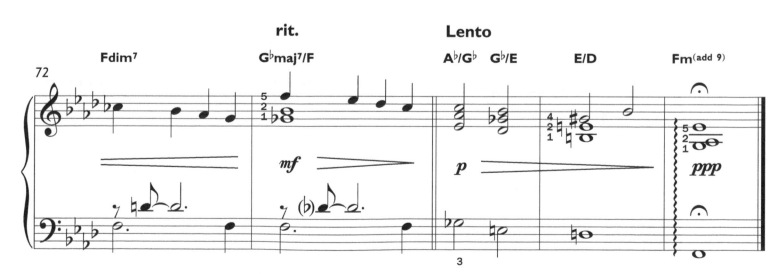

ANGELS

Words and Music by ROBERT PETER WILLIAMS
and GUY CHAMBERS

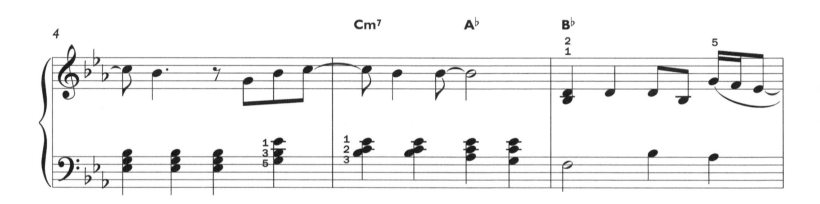

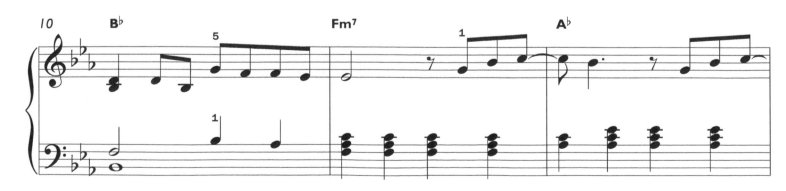

Coda

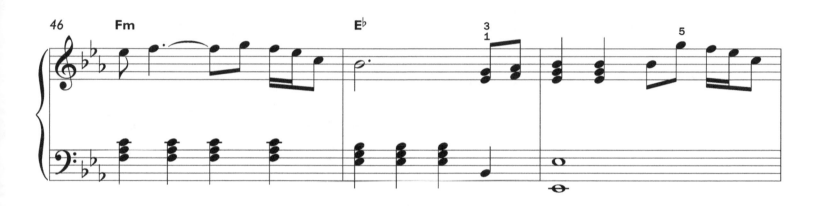

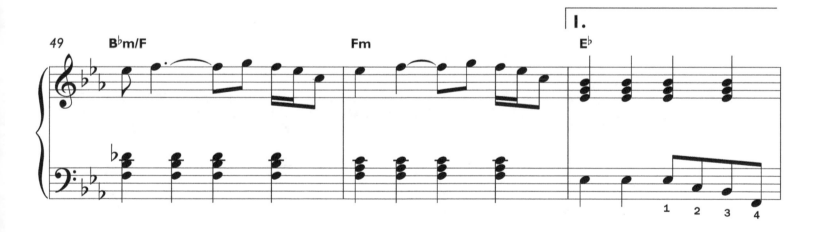

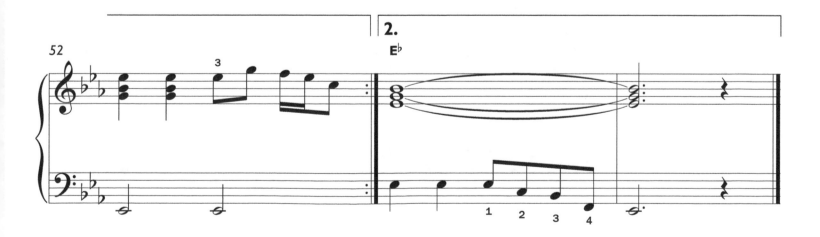

ANY OTHER NAME
from AMERICAN BEAUTY

Music by THOMAS NEWMAN

I. MAIN THEME

Freely (♩ = c.78)

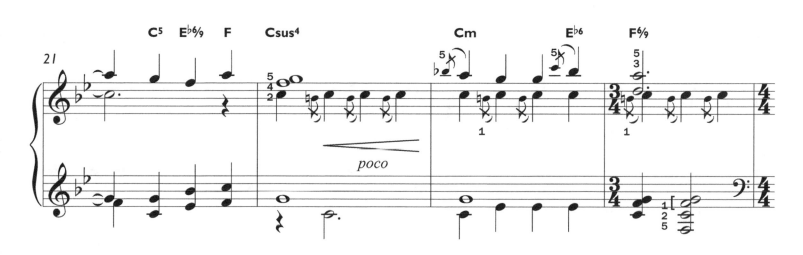

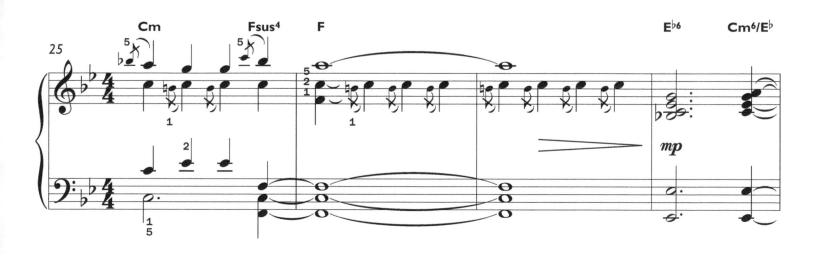

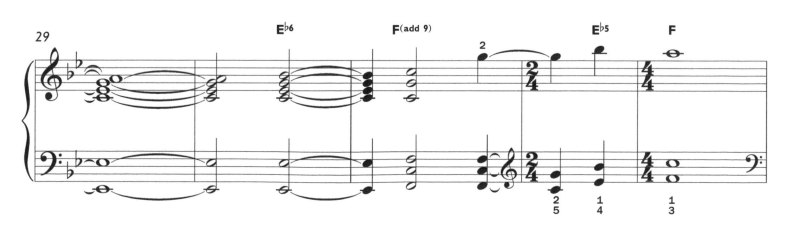

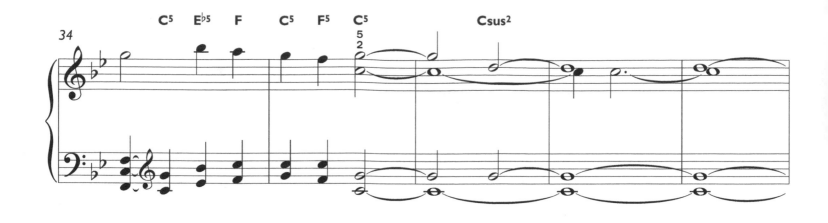

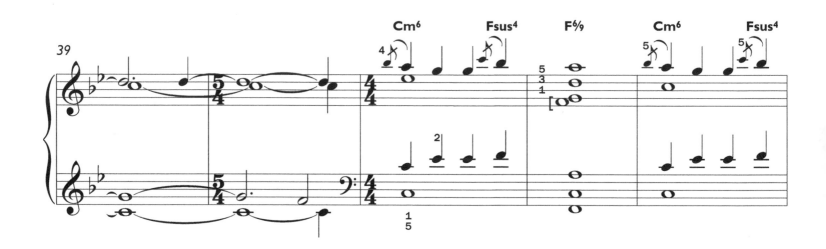

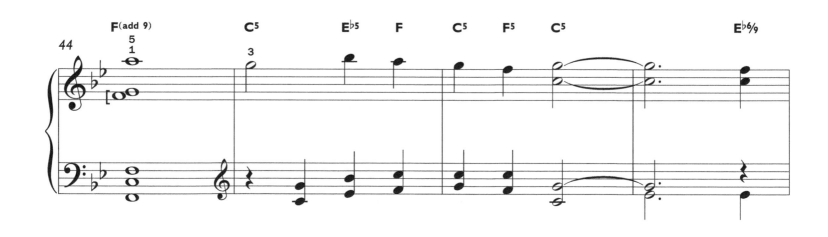

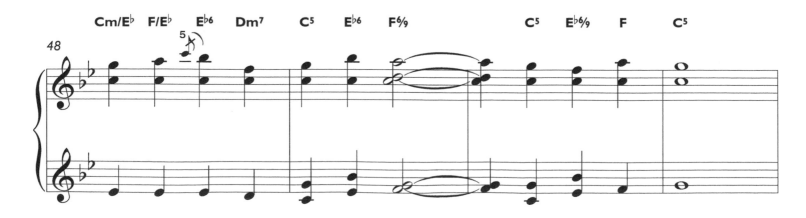

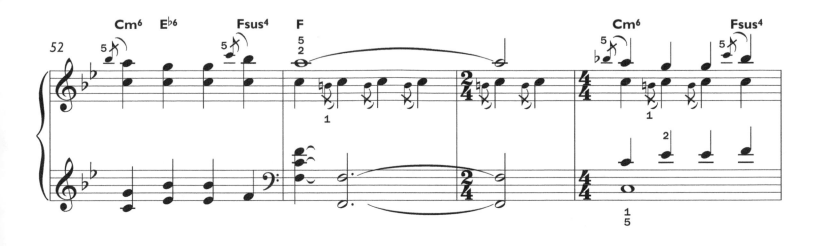

II. ANGELA UNDRESS

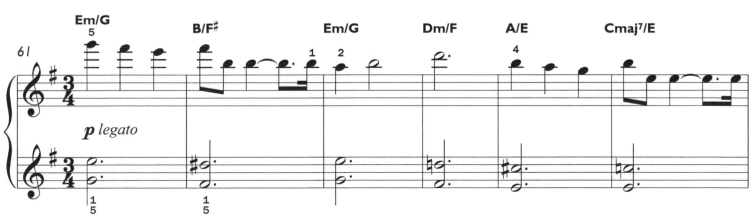

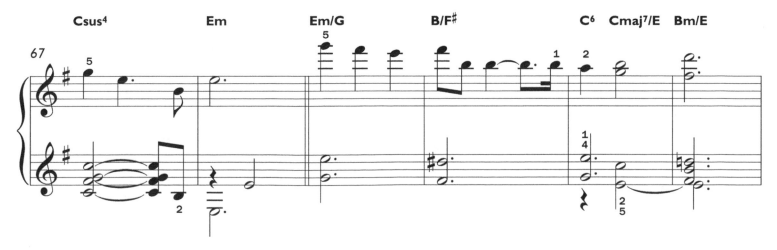

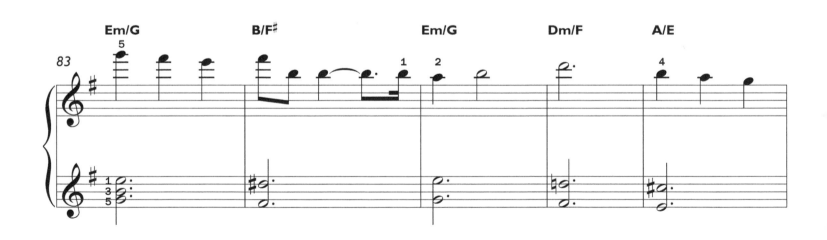

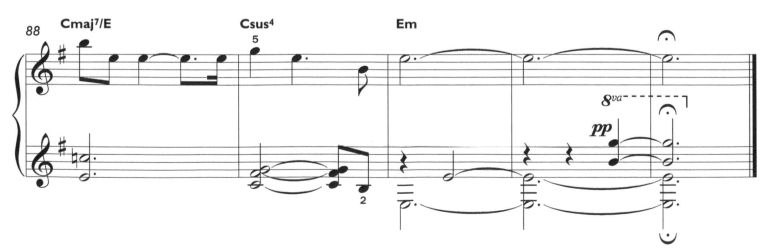

BEDSHAPED

Words and Music by TIM RICE-OXLEY,
RICHARD HUGHES, TOM CHAPLIN
and JAMES SANGER

Steadily, with expression ♩ = c.72

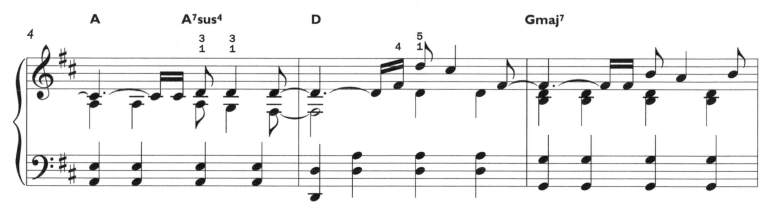

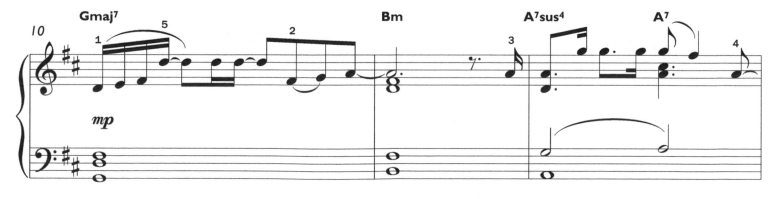

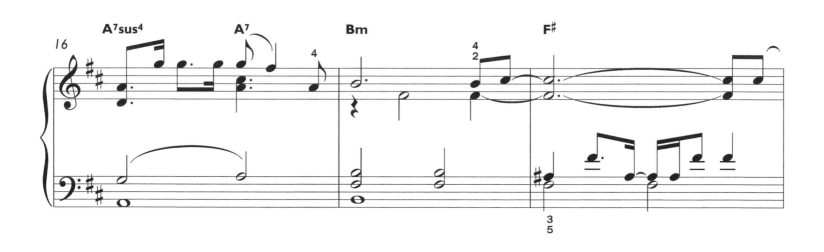

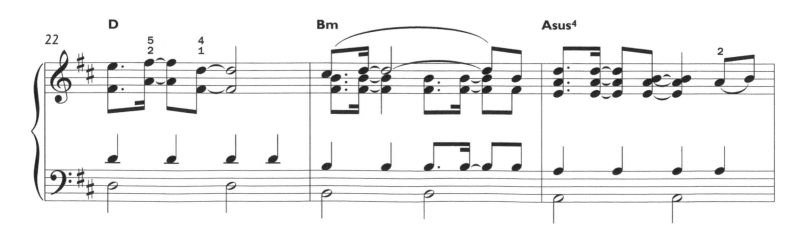

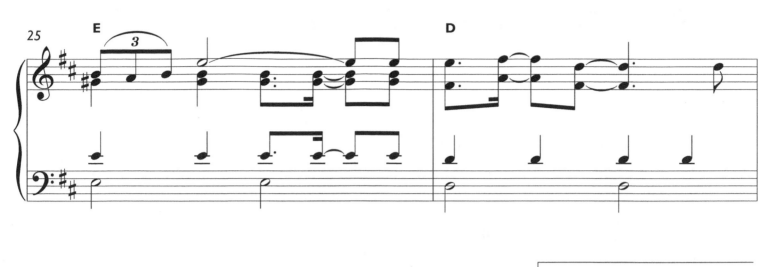

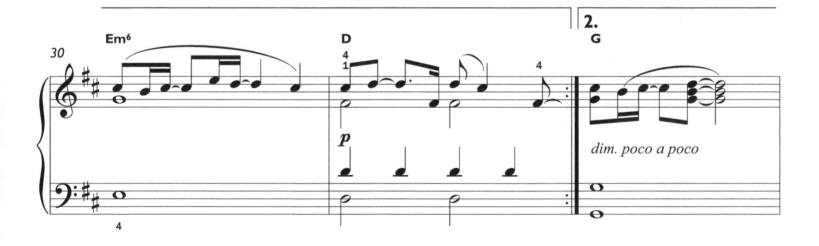

BRIDGE OVER TROUBLED WATER

Words and Music by PAUL SIMON

Moderately, like a spiritual

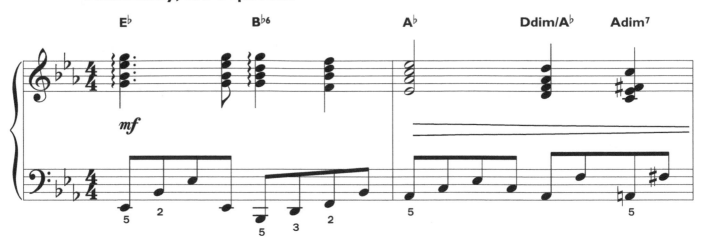

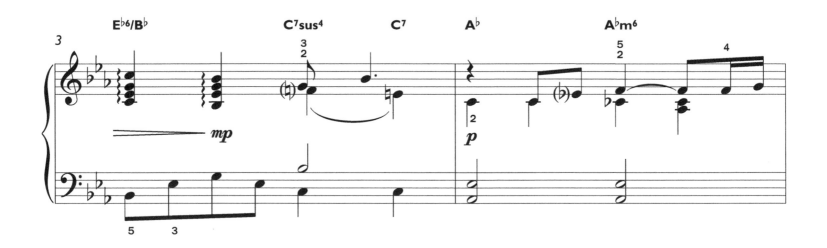

Rubato

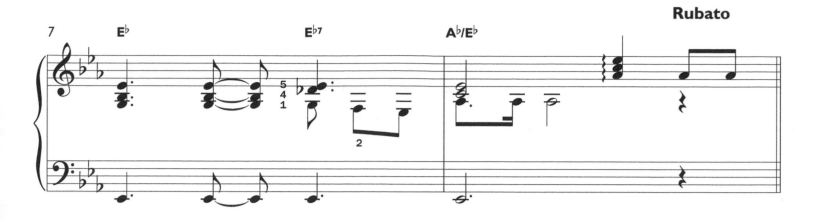

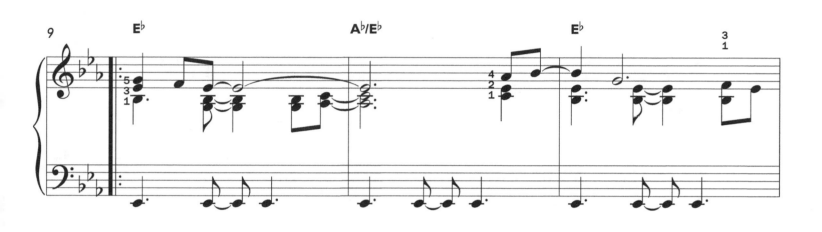

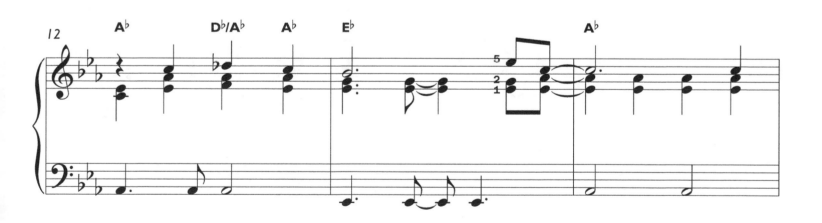

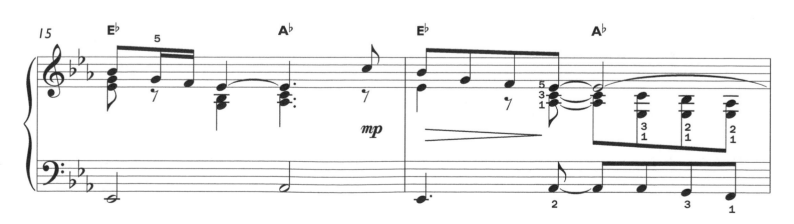

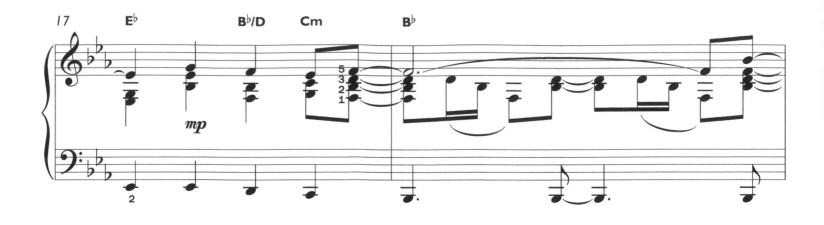

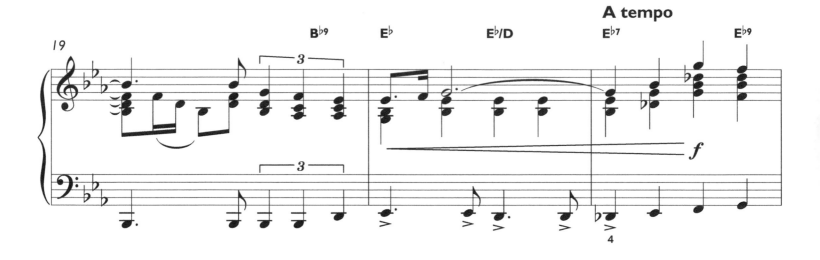

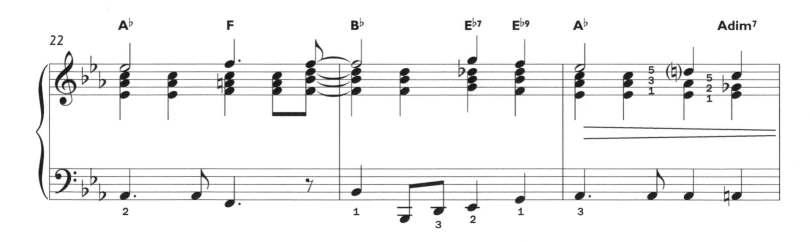

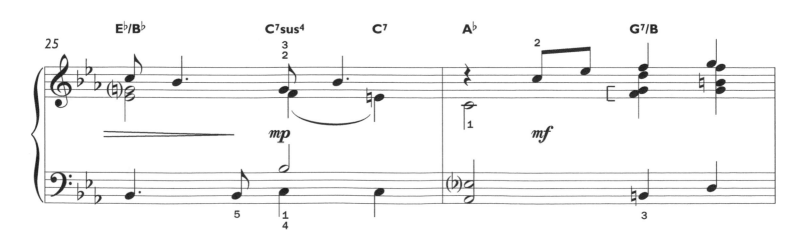

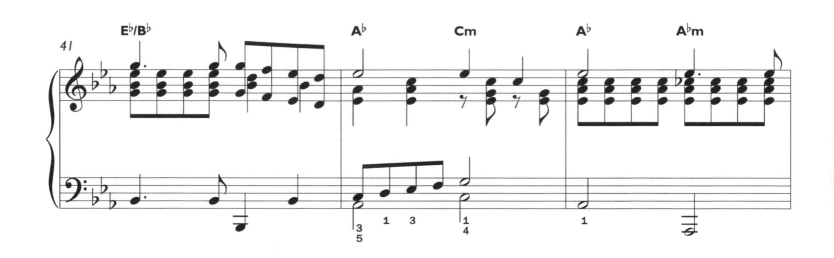

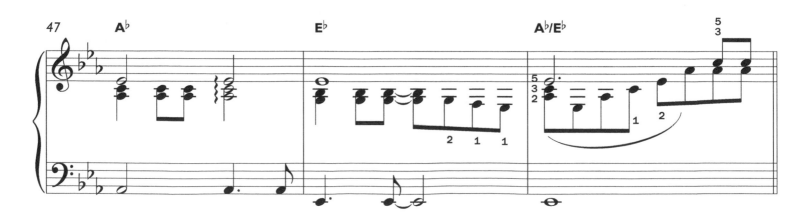

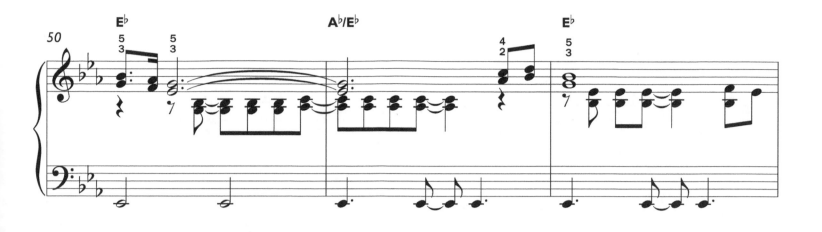

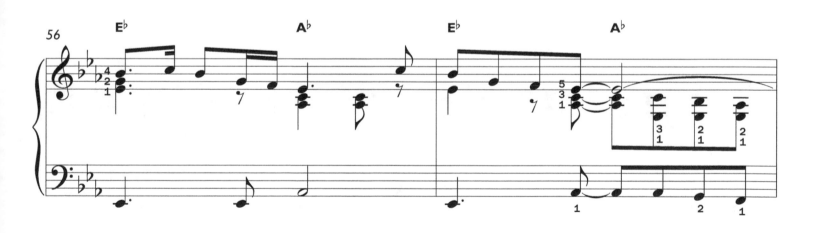

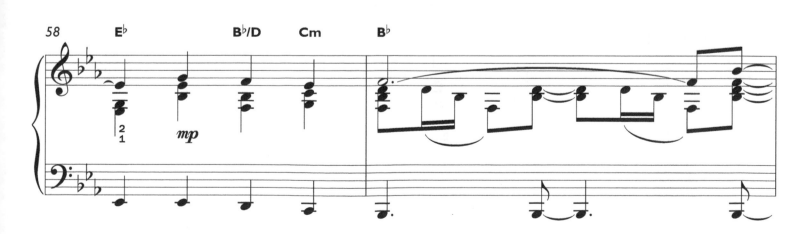

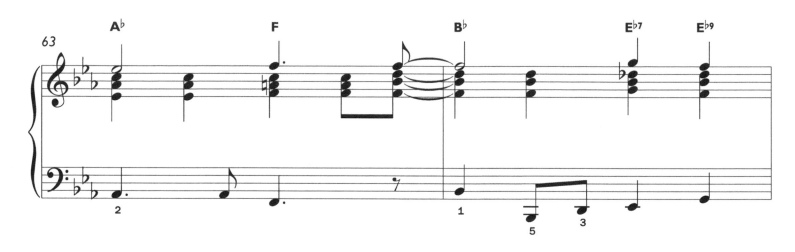

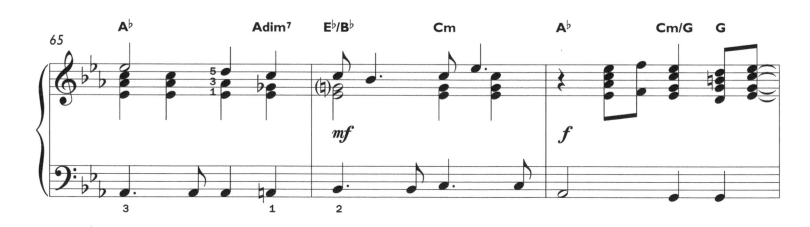

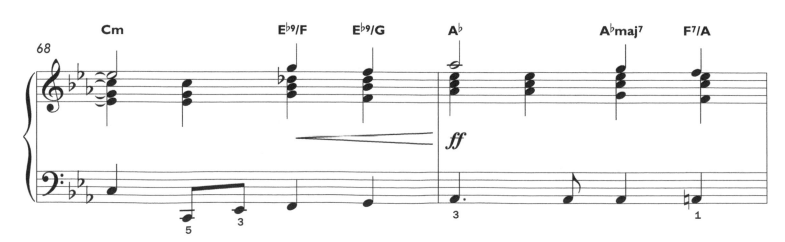

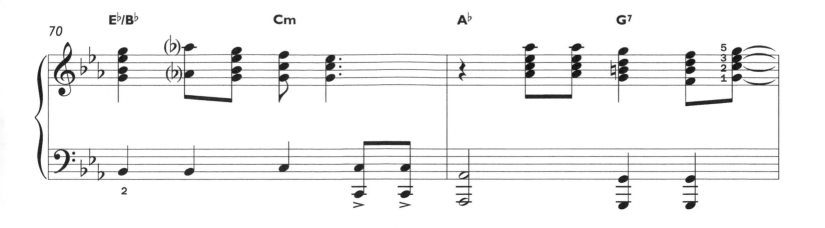

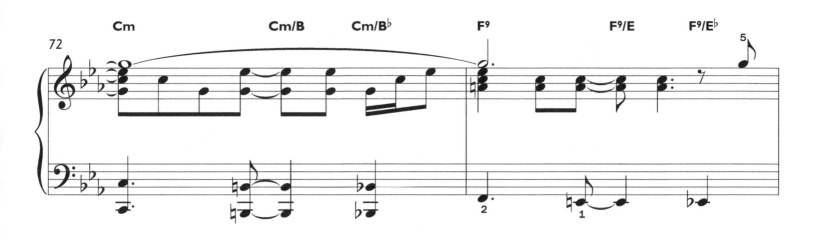

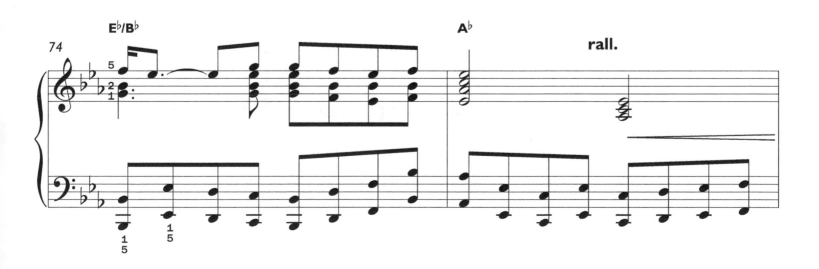

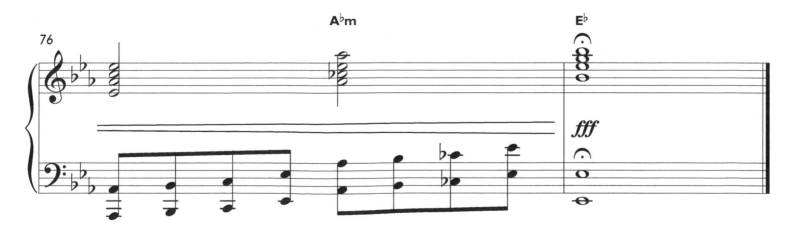

CLAIR DE LUNE

By CLAUDE DEBUSSY

Rubato

pp

cresc. et animé

D.C. al Fine

dim.

(They Long To Be)
CLOSE TO YOU

Lyric by HAL DAVID
Music by BURT BACHARACH

Slowly and steadily, with a swing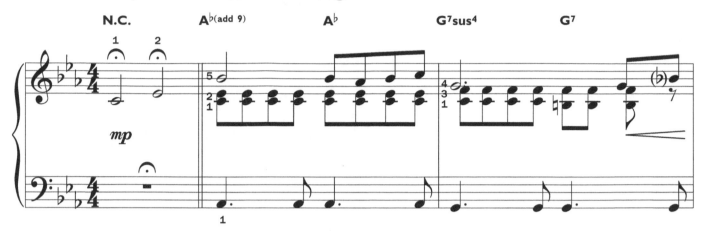

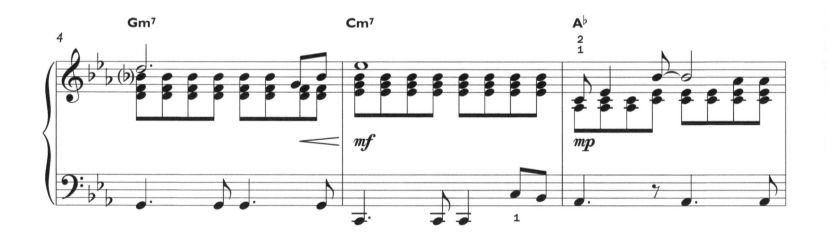

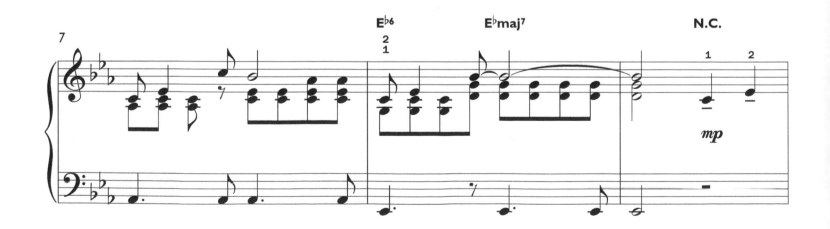

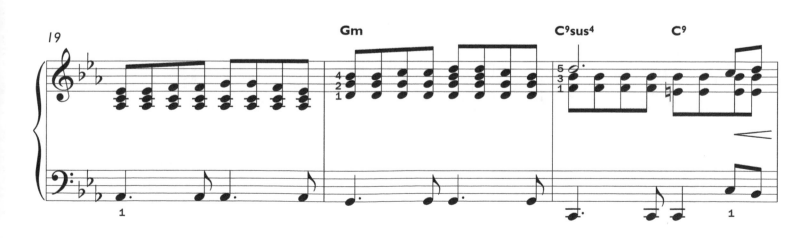

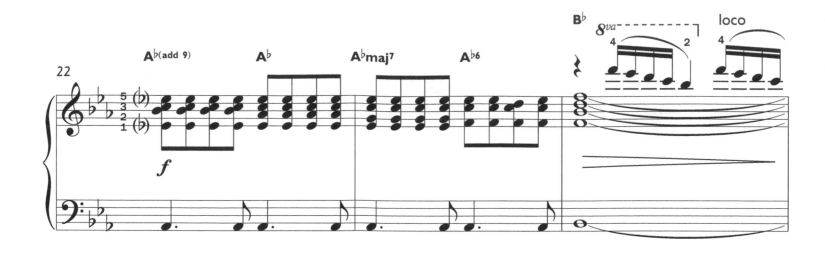

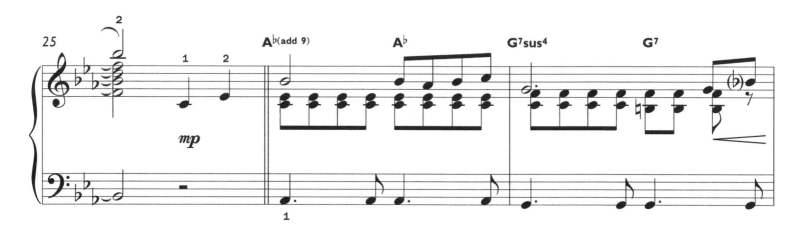

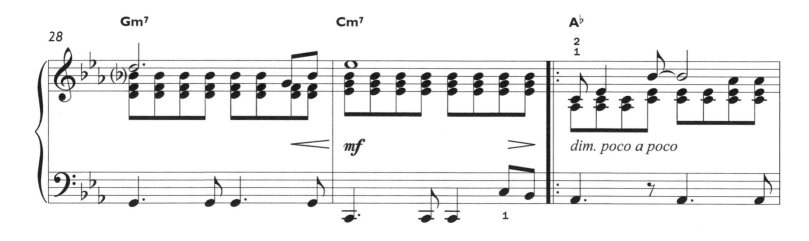

Repeat to fade

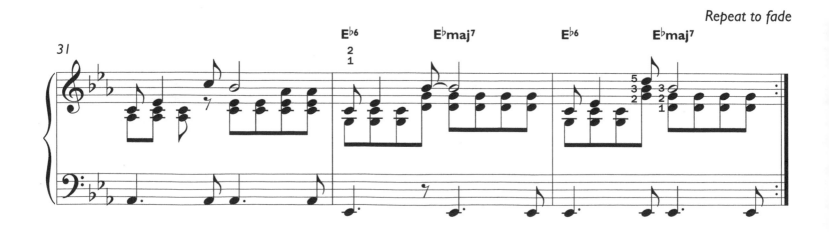

THE ENTERTAINER

By SCOTT JOPLIN

Steadily, not too fast

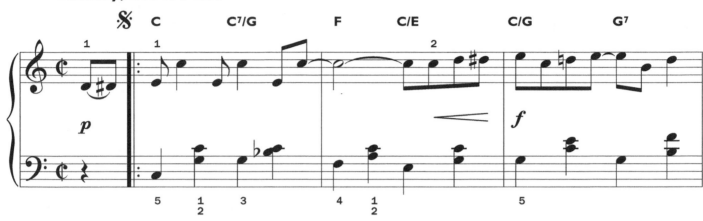

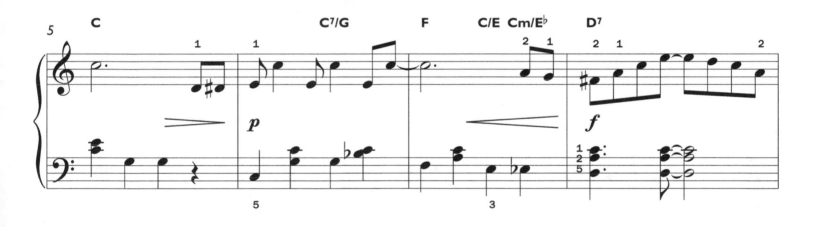

To Coda

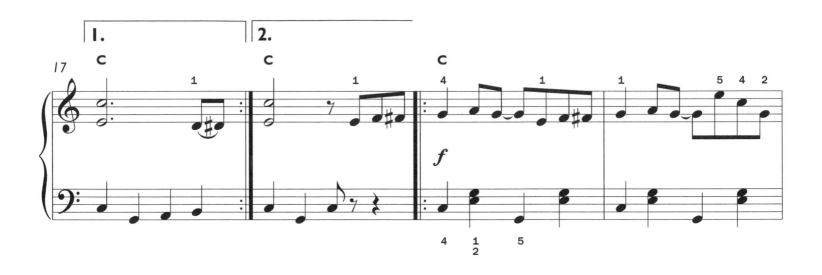

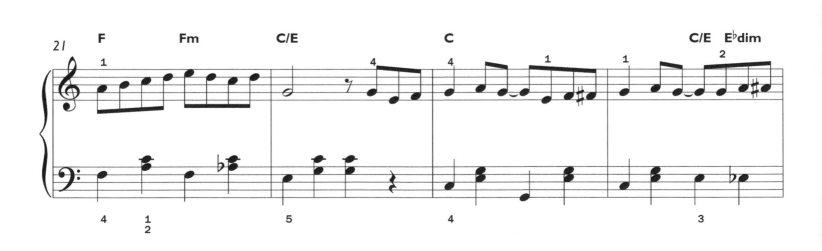

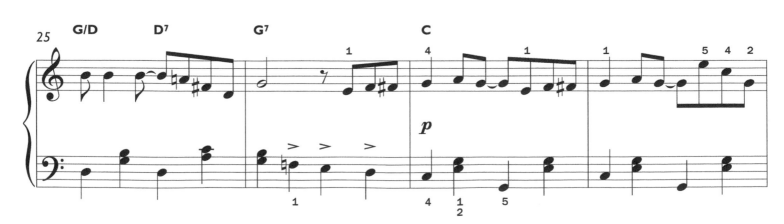

34

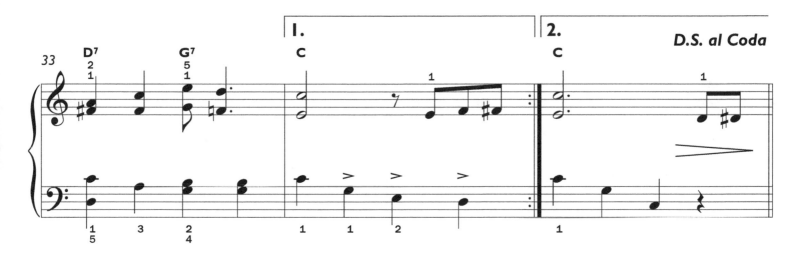

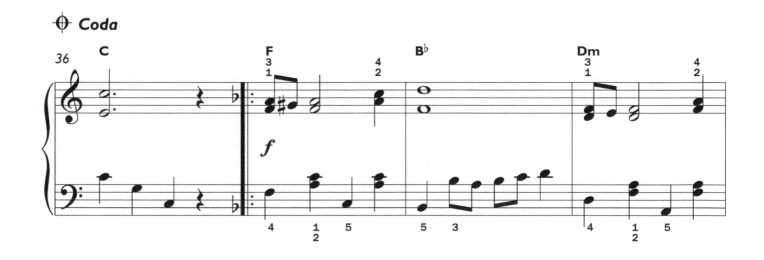

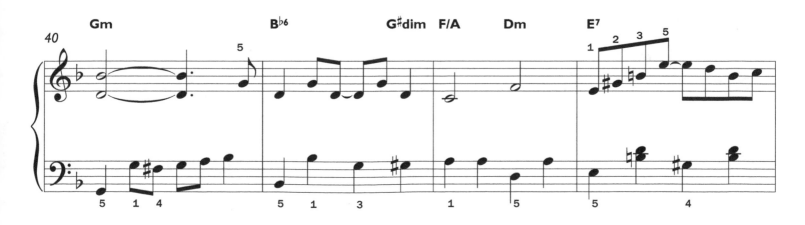

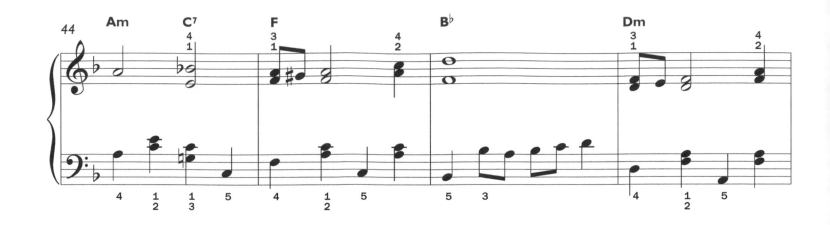

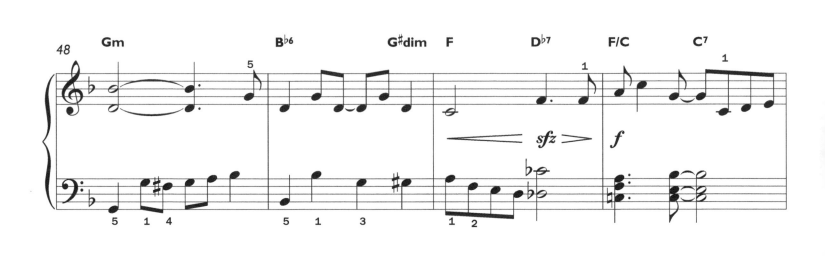

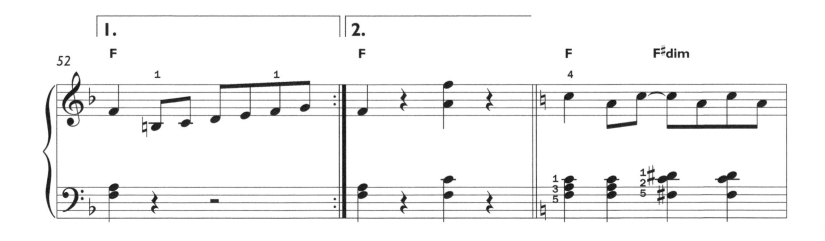

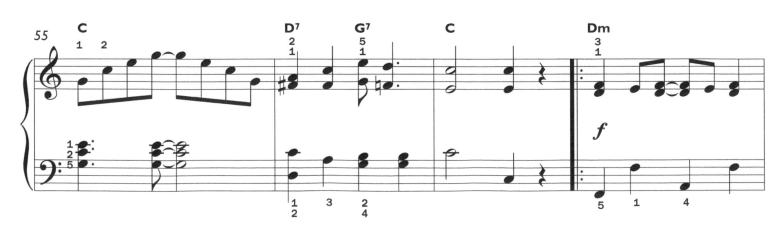

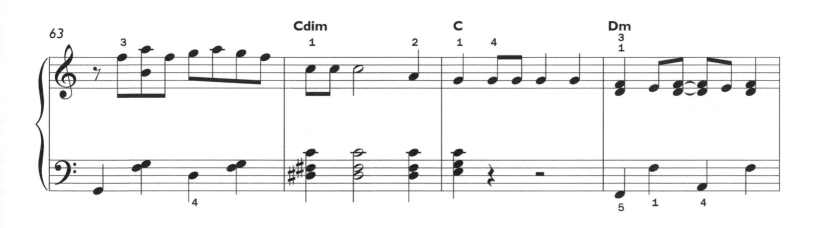

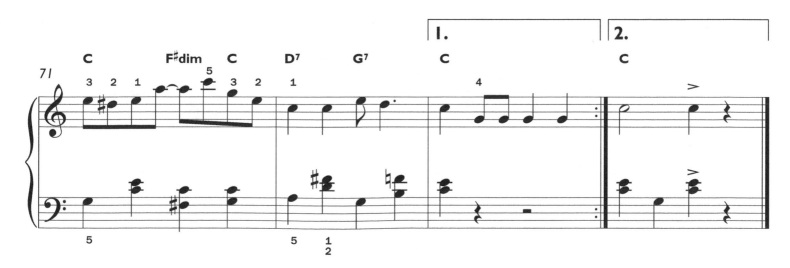

DON'T KNOW WHY

Words and Music by JESSE HARRIS

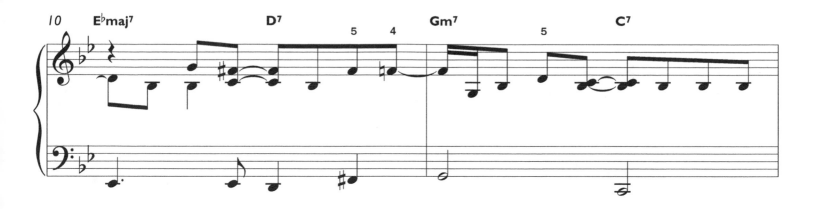

To Coda ⊕

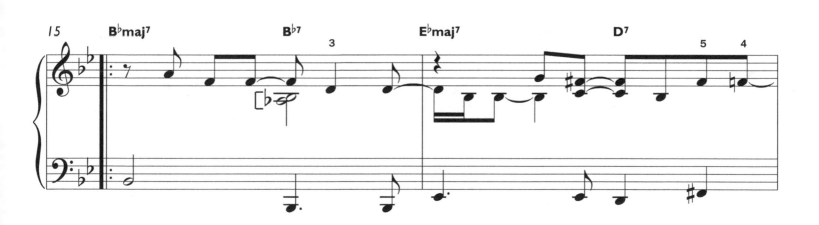

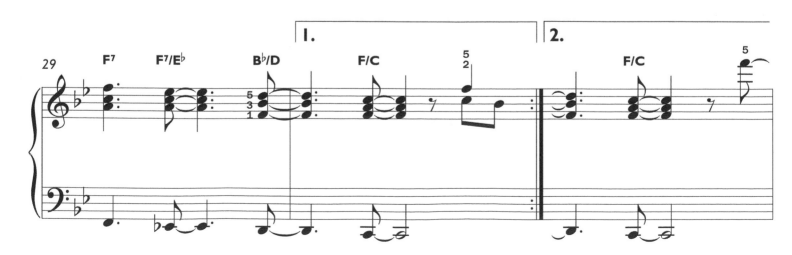

D.S. al Coda

Coda

FUR ELISE

By LUDWIG VAN BEETHOVEN

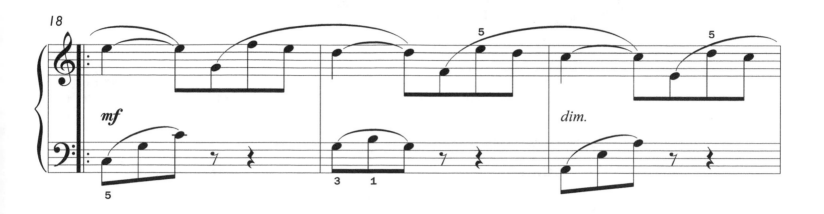

GEORGIA ON MY MIND

Words by STUART GORRELL
Music by HOAGY CARMICHAEL

Moderately, with a blues feel ♩ = 60

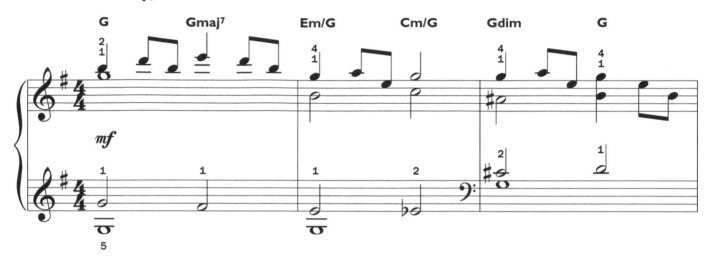

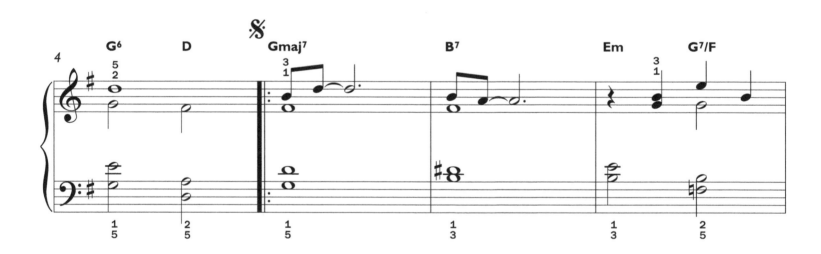

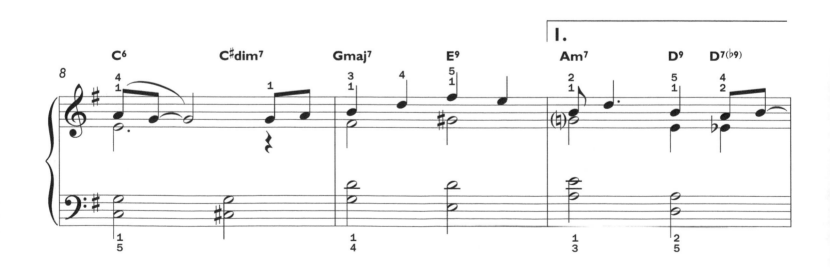

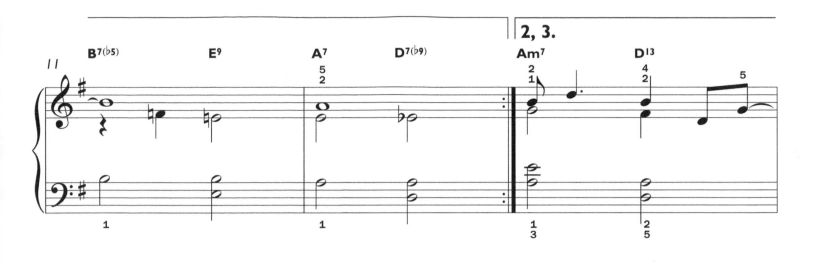

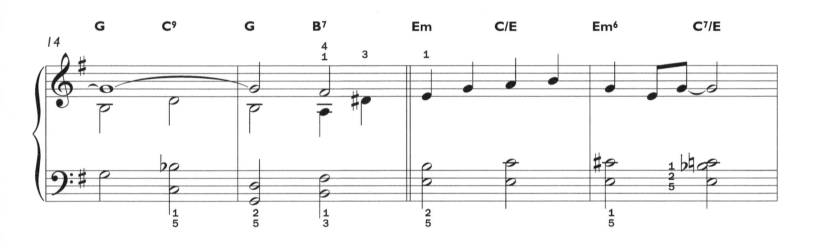

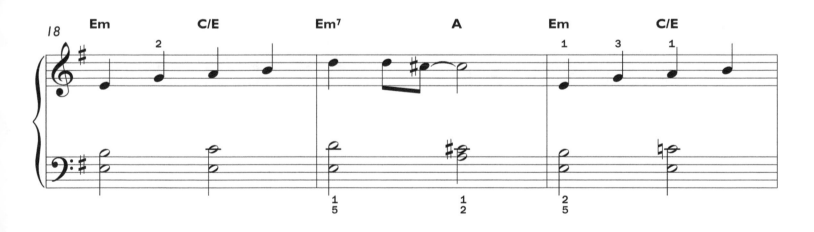

D.S. al Fine

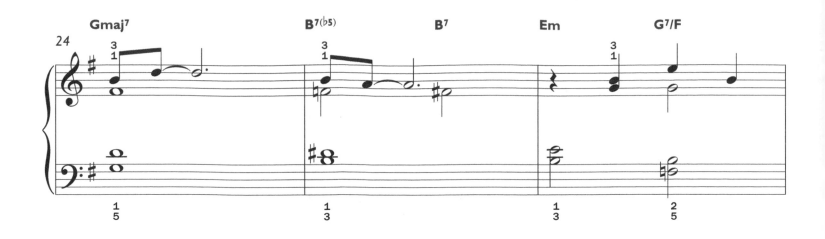

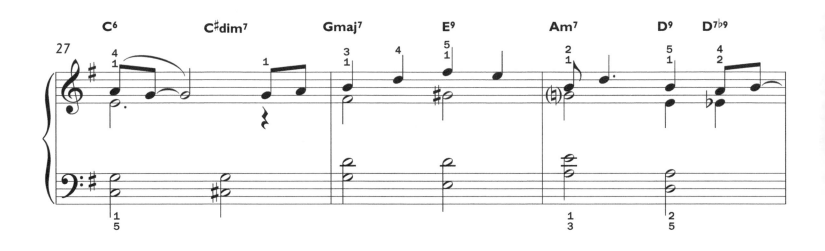

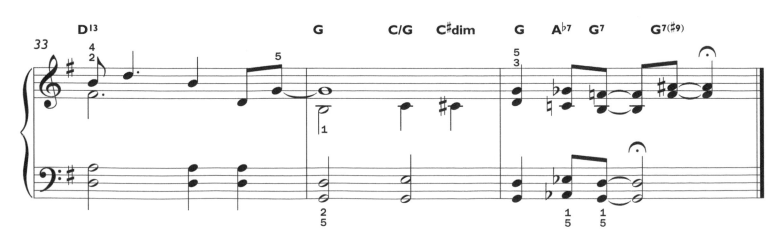

GYMNOPEDIE NO. 1

By ERIK SATIE

Adagio

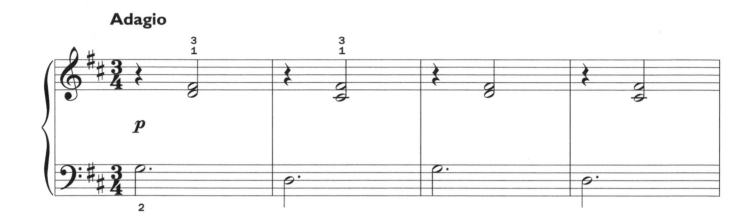

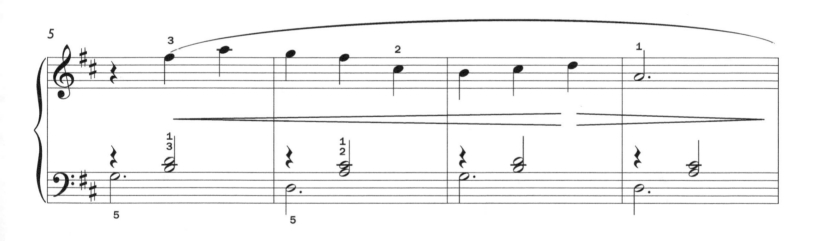

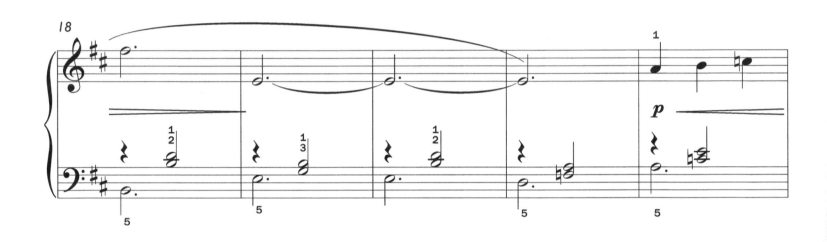

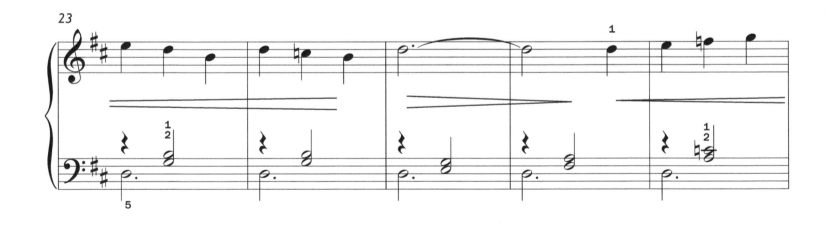

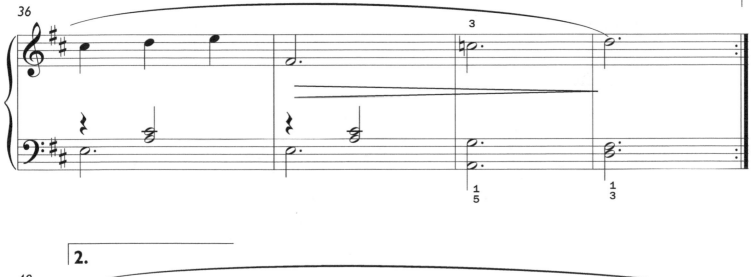

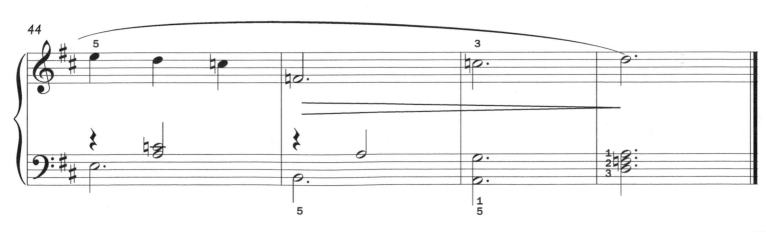

THE HEART ASKS PLEASURE FIRST
from THE PIANO

By MICHAEL NYMAN

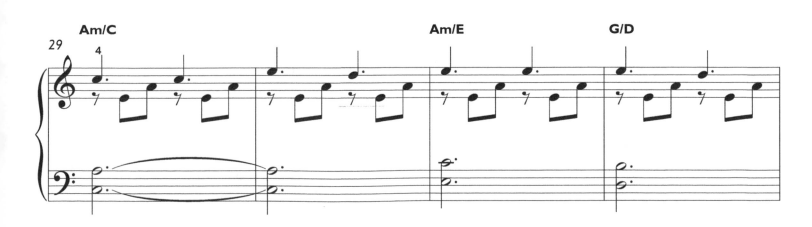

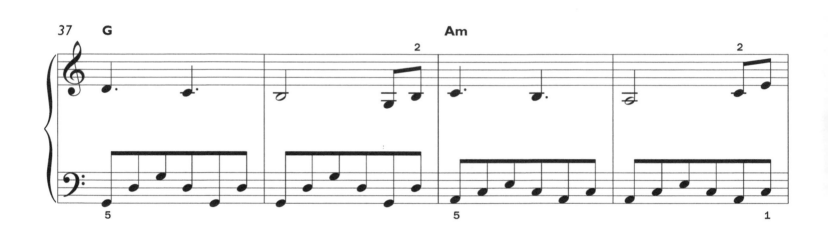

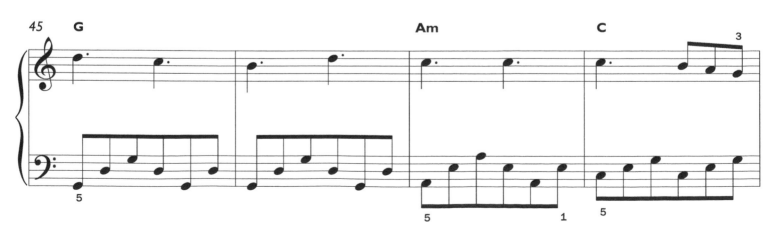

HOW TO SAVE A LIFE

Words and Music by JOSEPH KING
and ISAAC SLADE

Expressively ♩ = 124

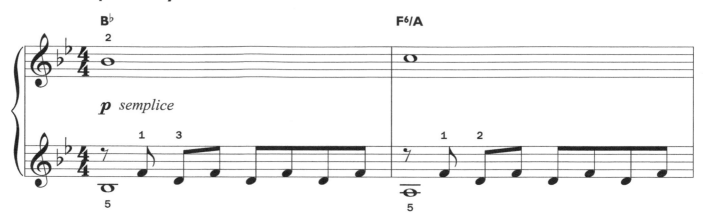

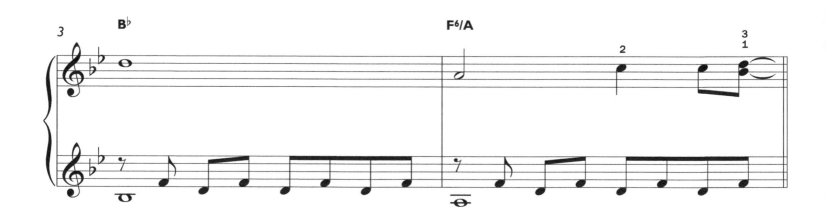

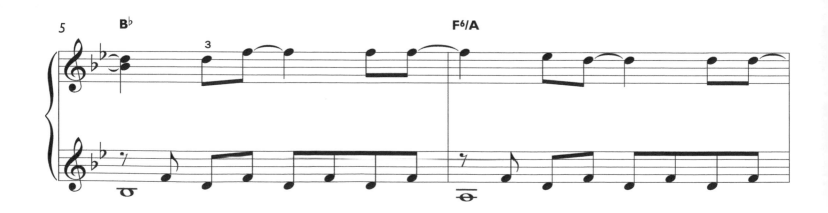

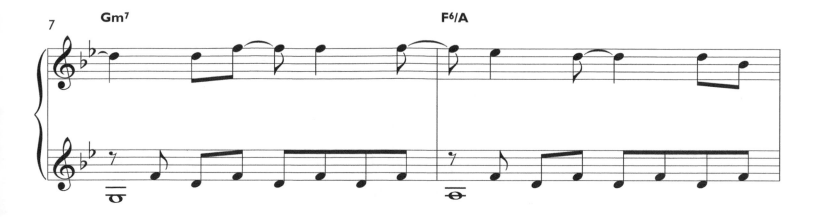

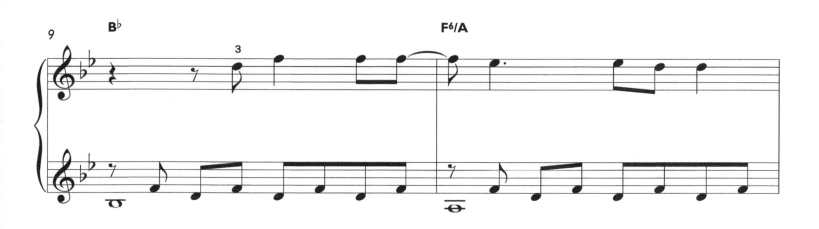

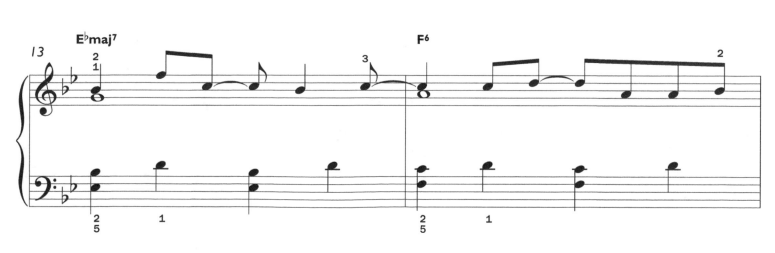

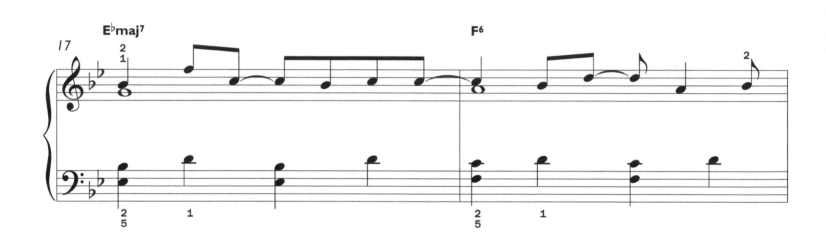

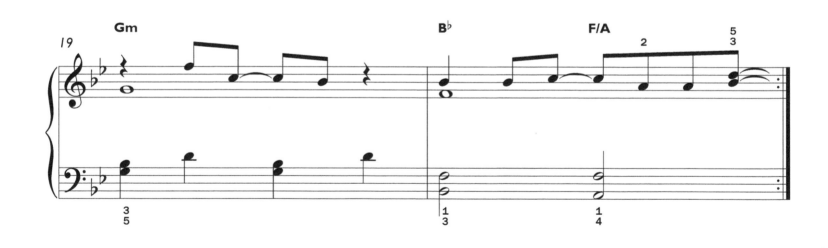

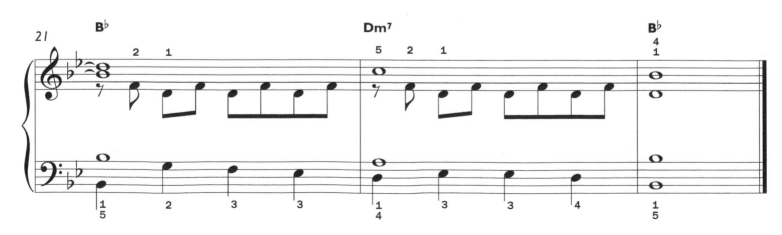

IN YOUR OWN SWEET WAY

By DAVE BRUBECK

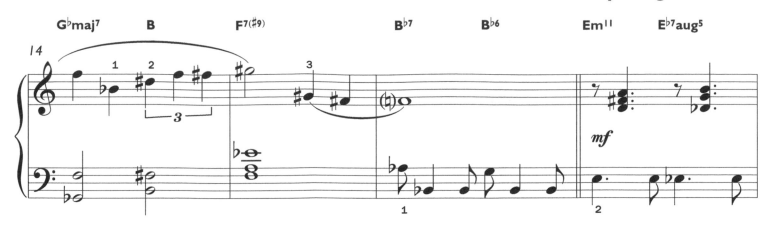

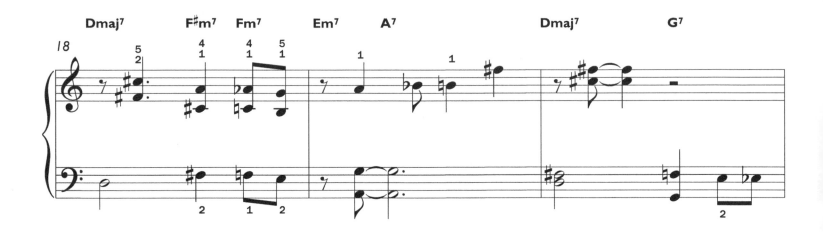

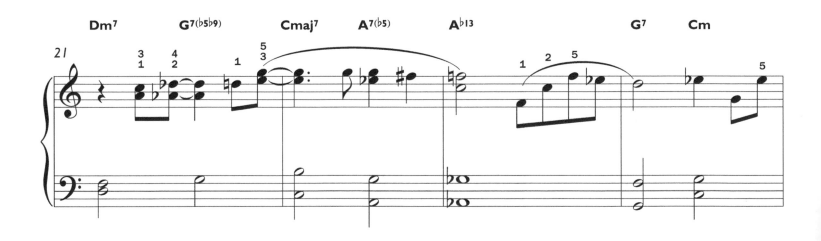

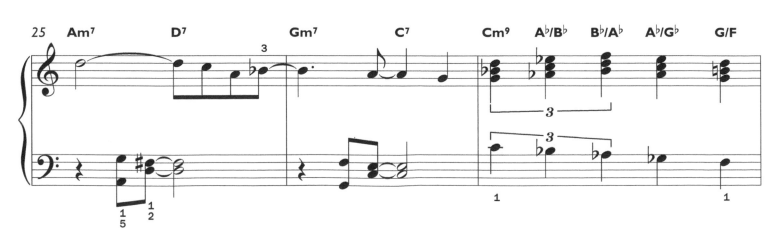

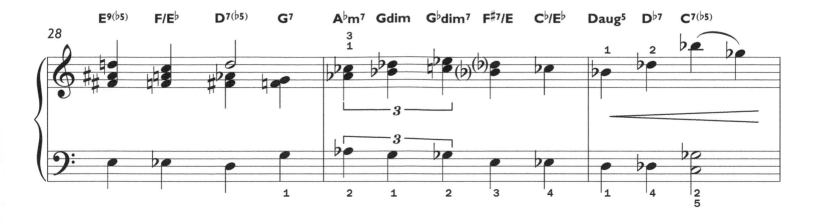

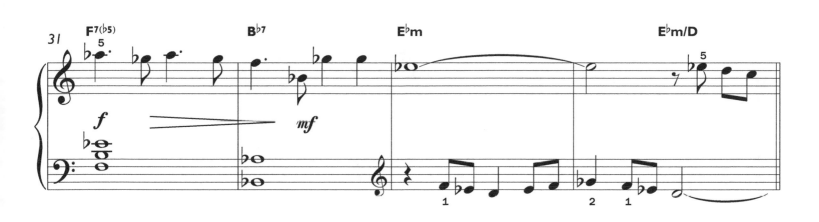

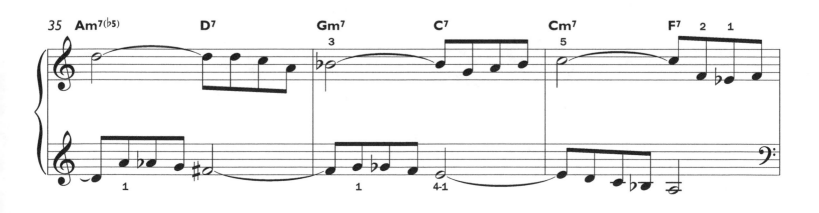

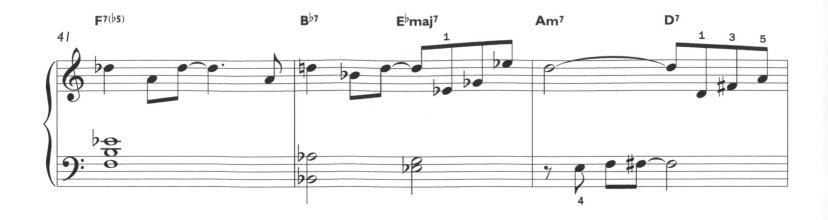

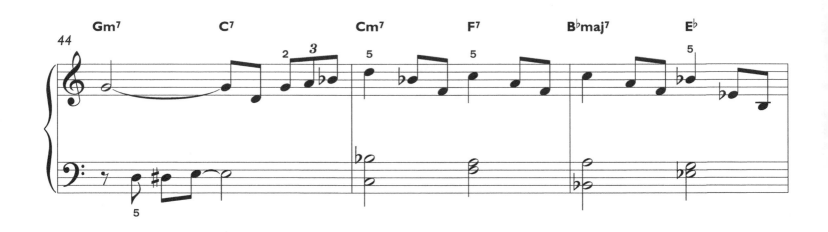

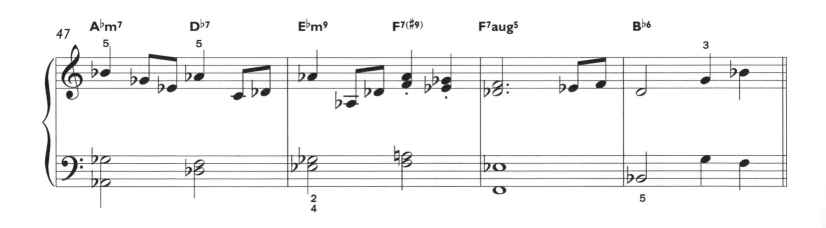

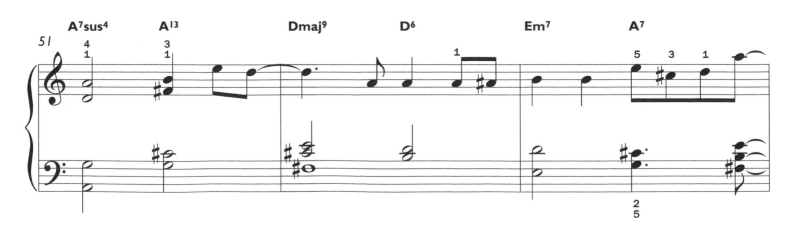

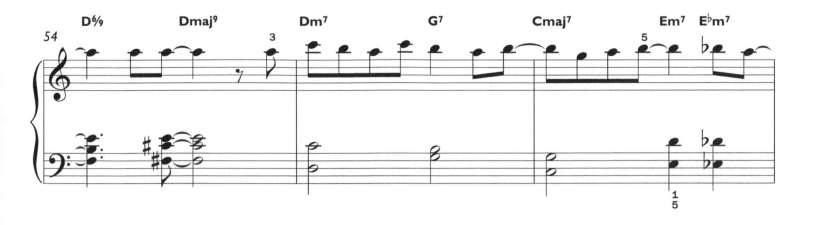

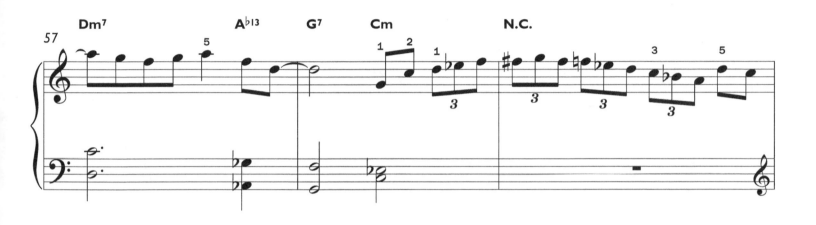

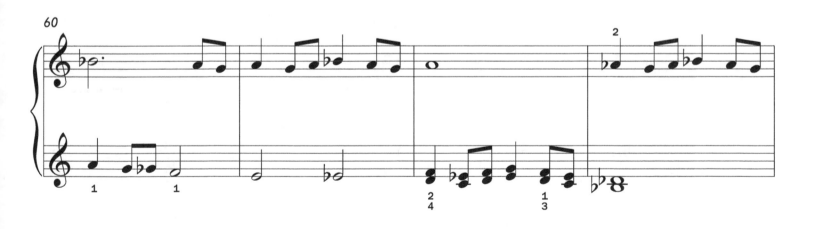

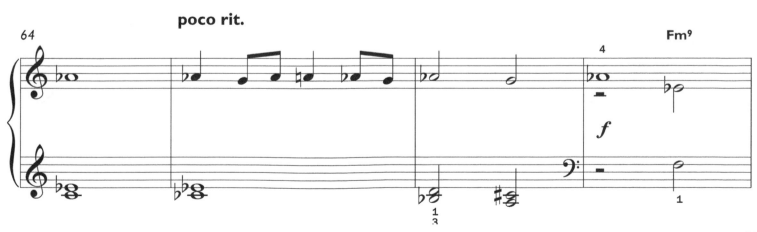

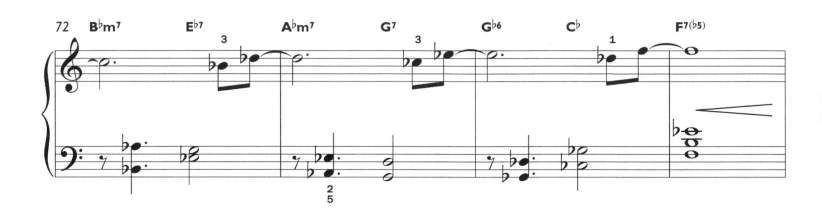

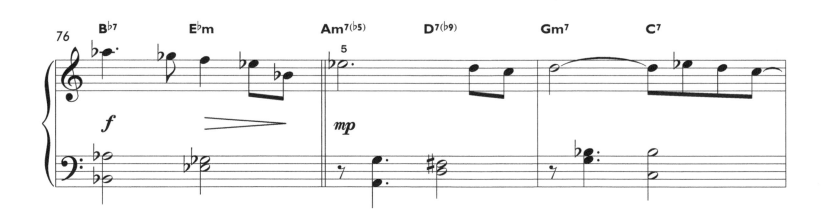

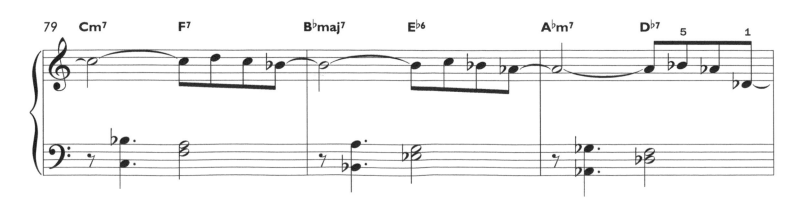

Like a waltz

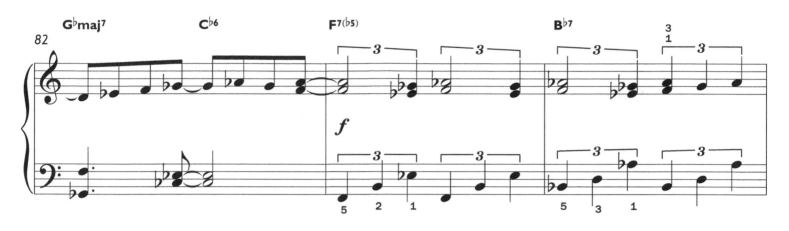

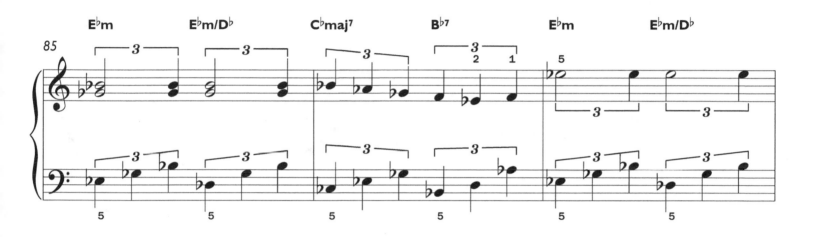

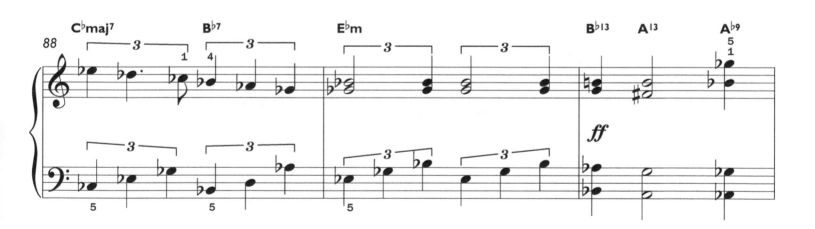

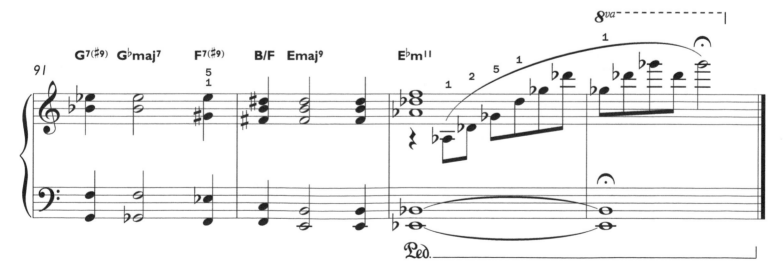

INTERMEZZO IN B MINOR, OP.119

By JOHANNES BRAHMS

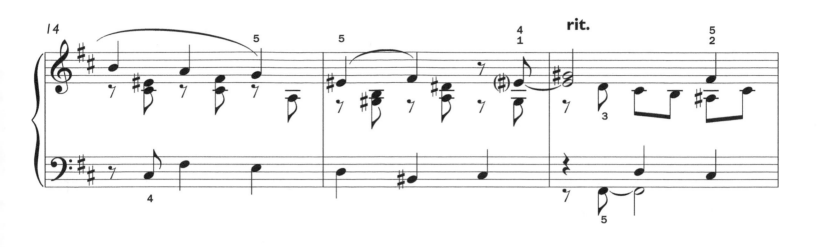

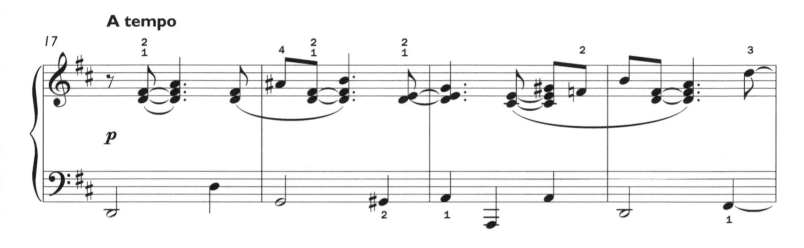

LA VALSE D'AMELIE

from AMELIE

By YANN TIERSEN

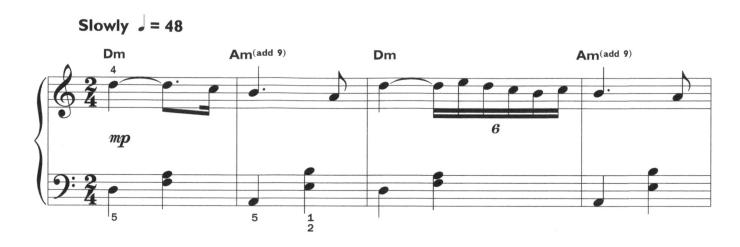

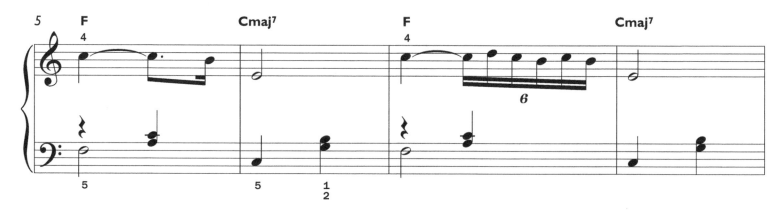

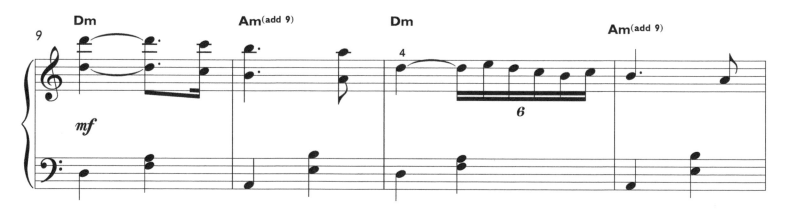

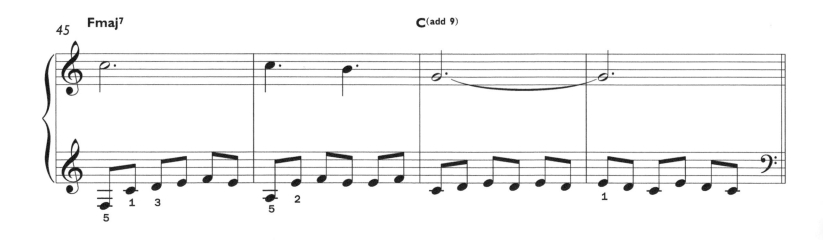

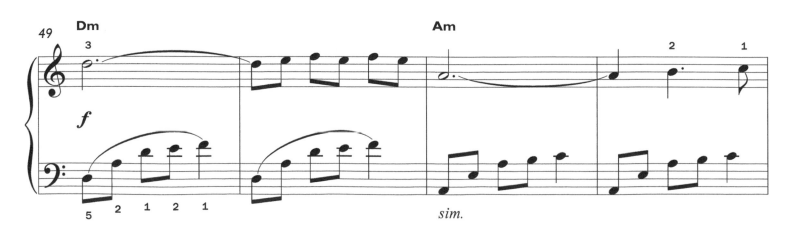

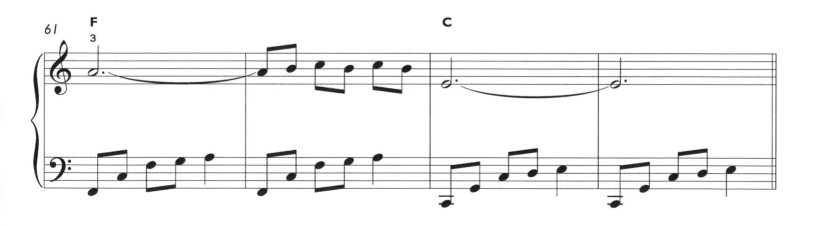

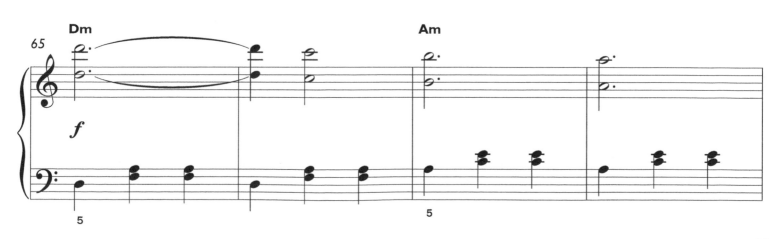

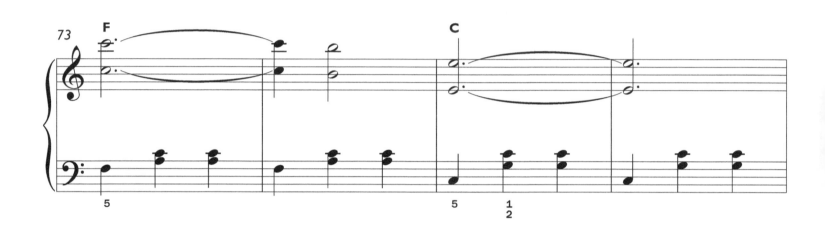

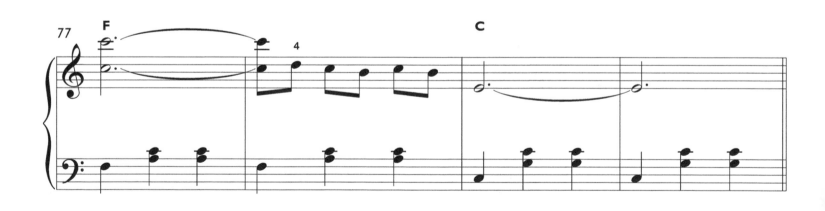

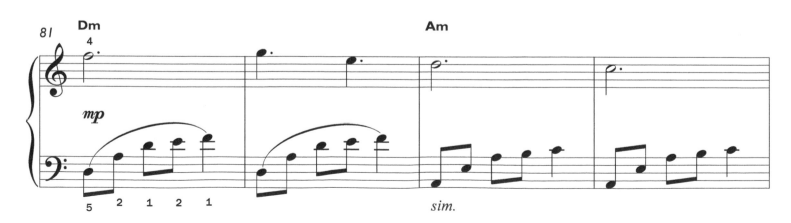

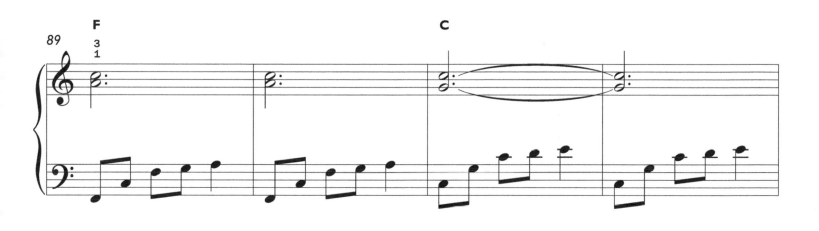

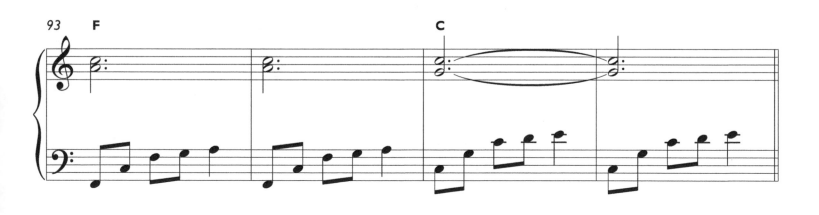

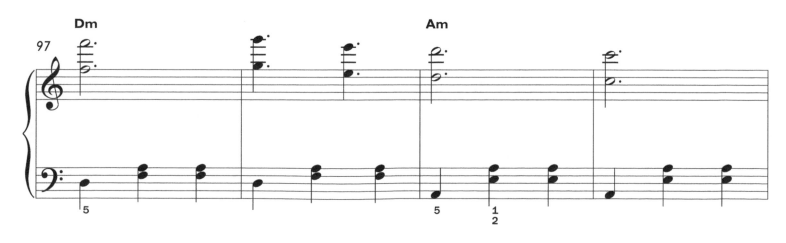

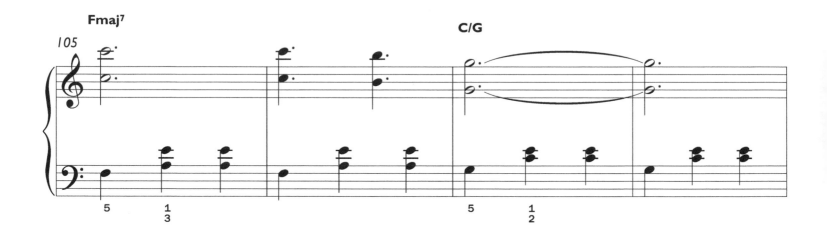

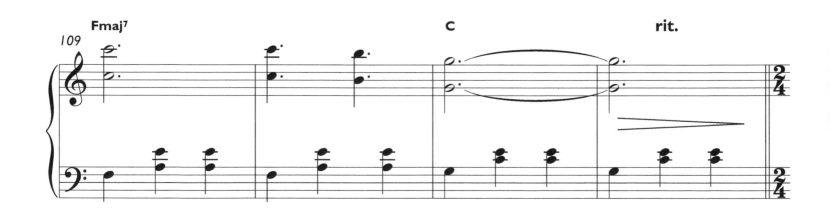

Slowly, Tempo Primo

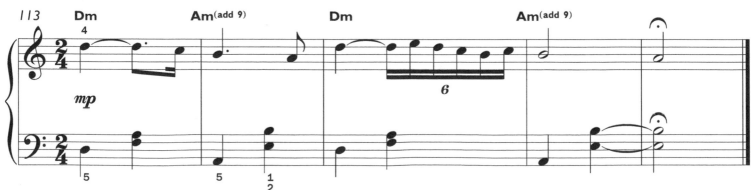

LET IT BE

Words and Music by JOHN LENNON
and PAUL McCARTNEY

Slowly

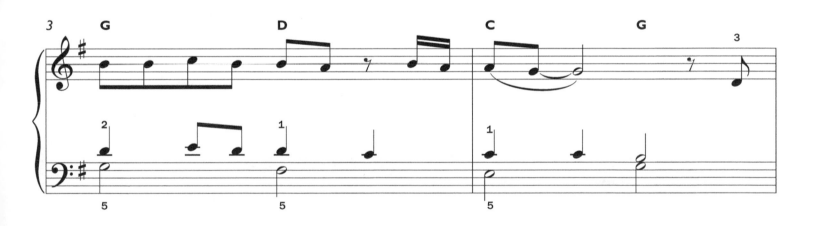

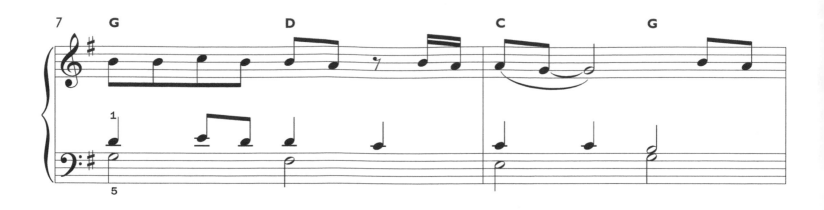

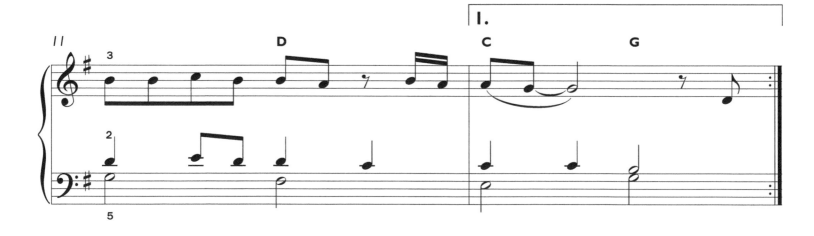

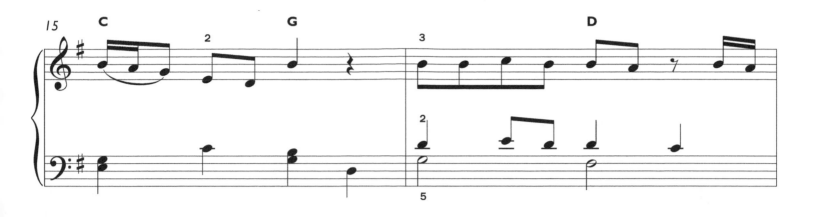

To Coda ⊕

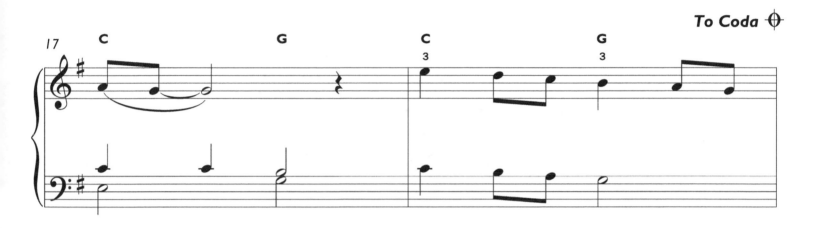

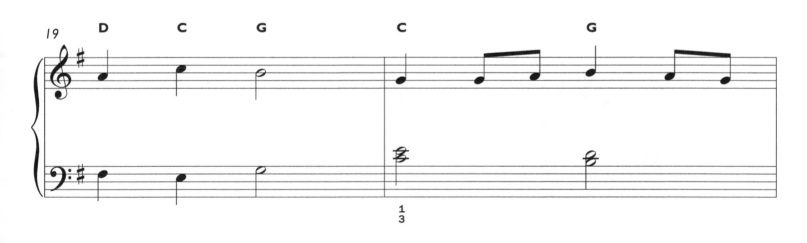

D.S. al Coda   ⊕ Coda

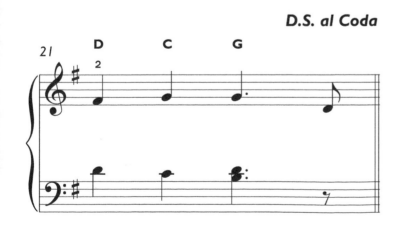
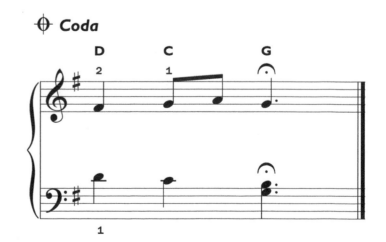

LE ONDE

By LUDOVICO EINAUDI

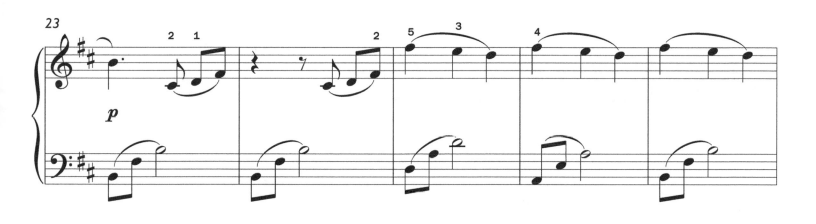

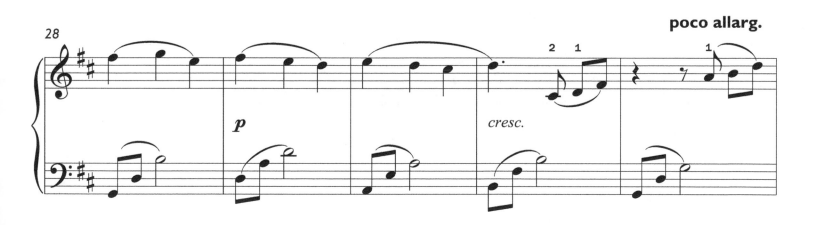

poco tratt.
poco allarg.
A tempo

sim.

poco tratt. A tempo

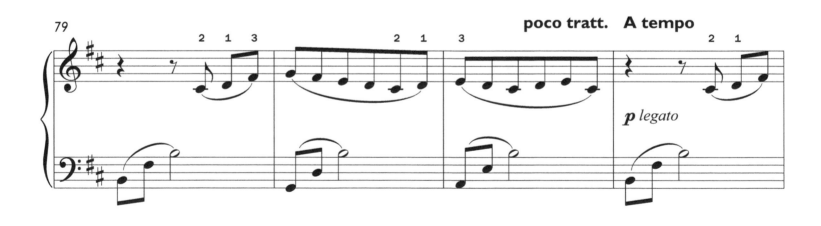

A tempo

allarg.

A tempo

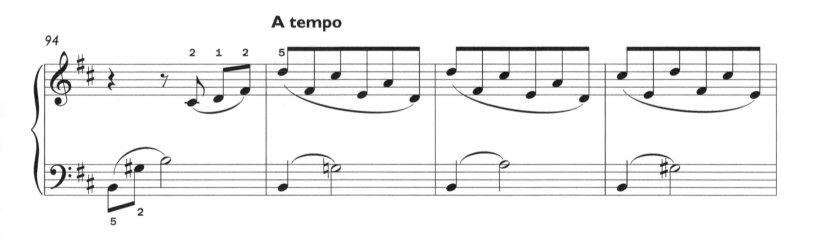

allarg.

A tempo

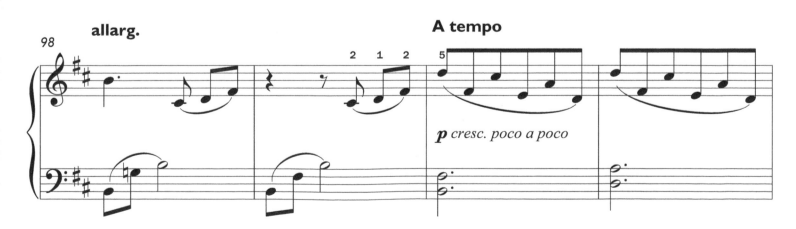

p cresc. poco a poco

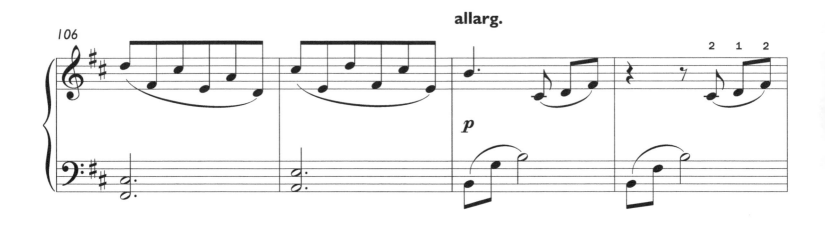

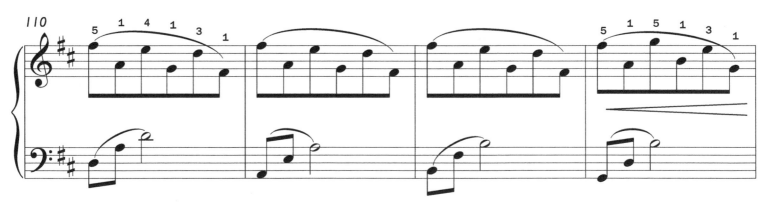

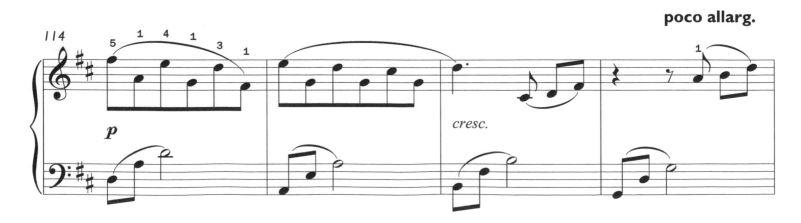

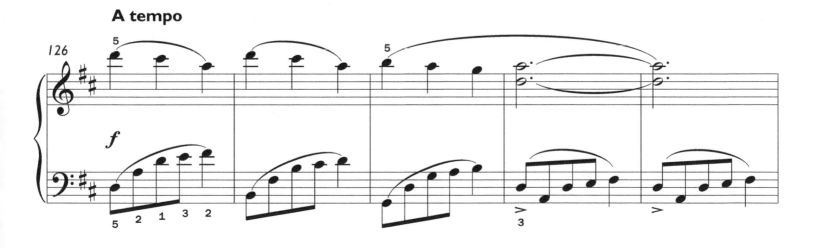

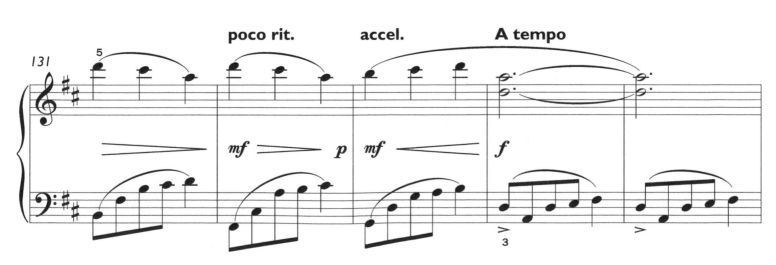

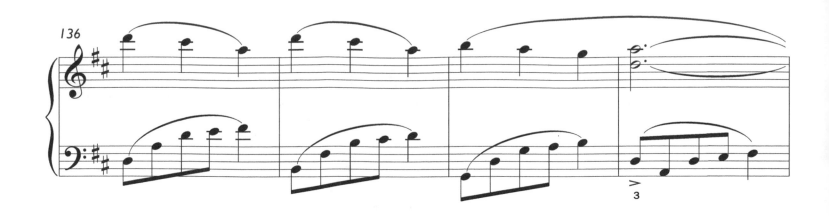

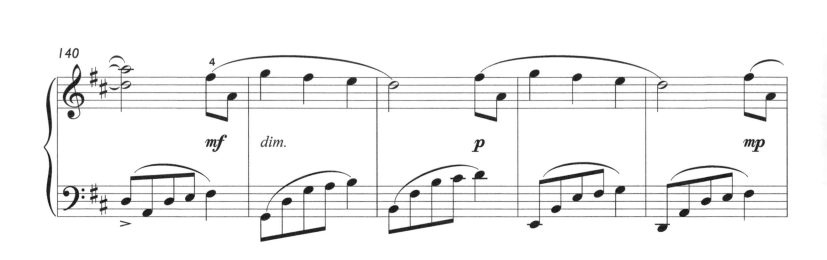

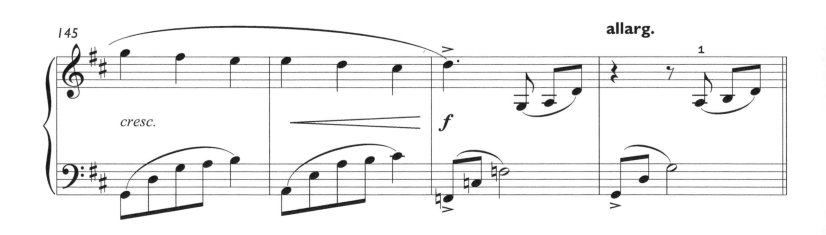

poco tratt.

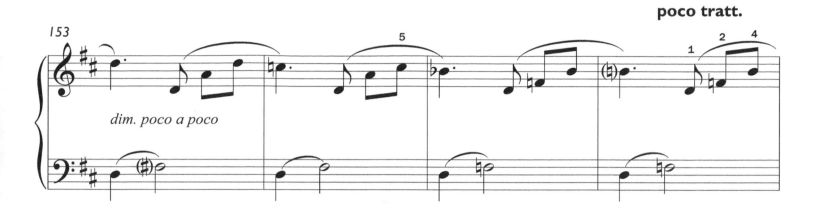

poco tratt.

poco tratt.

molto rall.

LES MARIONETTES

By ZBIGNIEW PREISNER

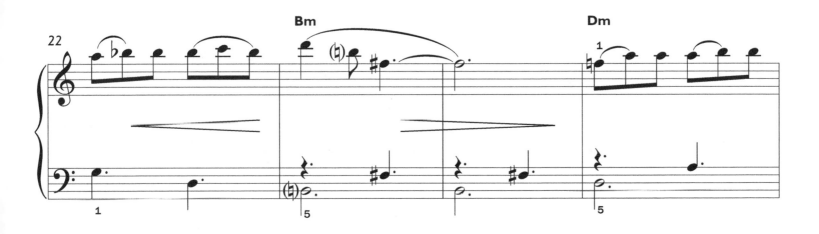

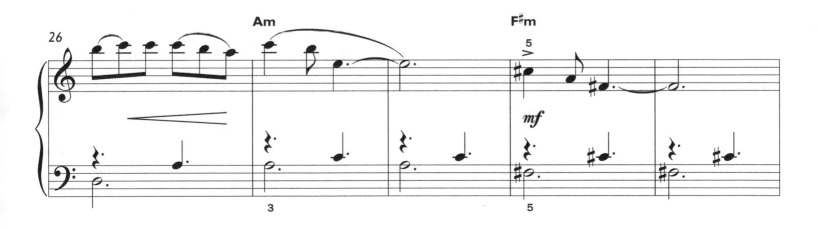

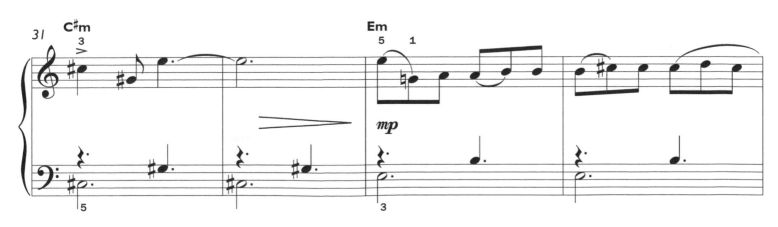

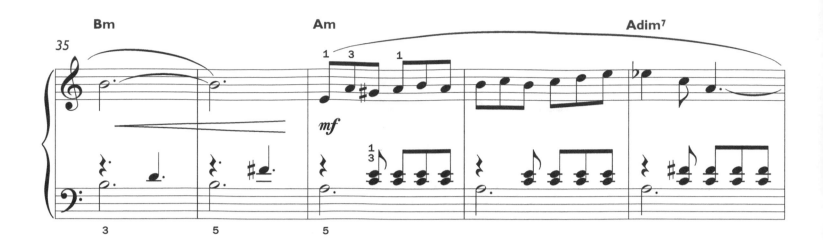

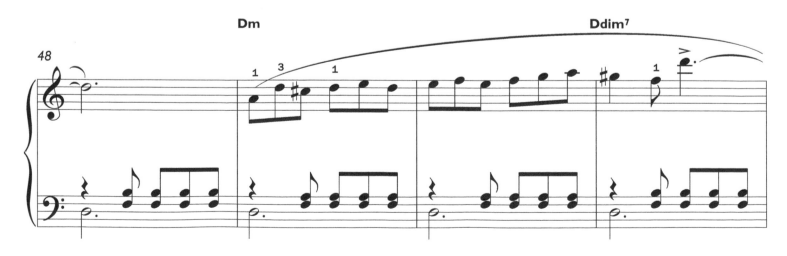

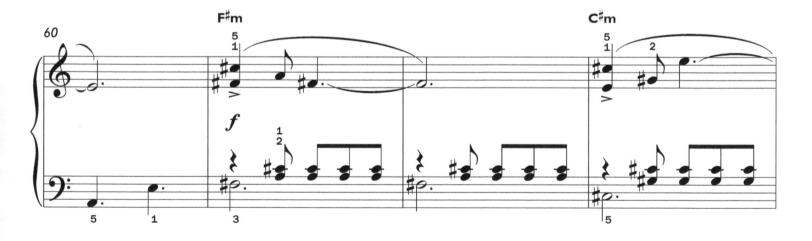

LIEBESTRAUM
(Dream Of Love)

By FRANZ LISZT

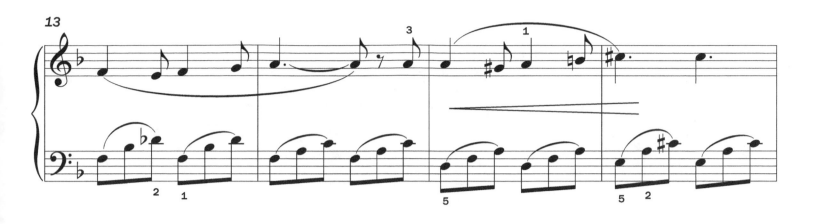

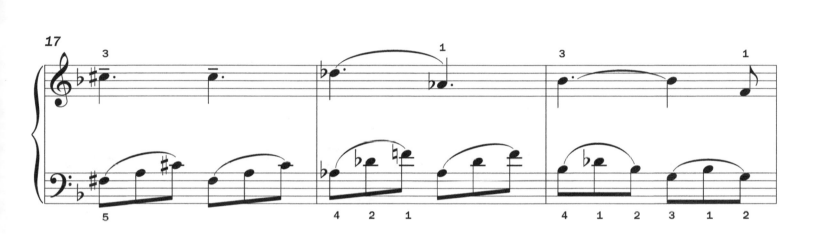

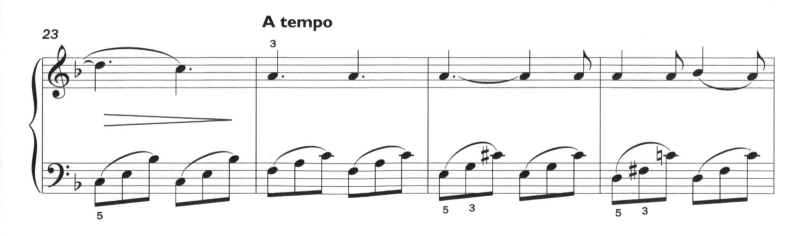

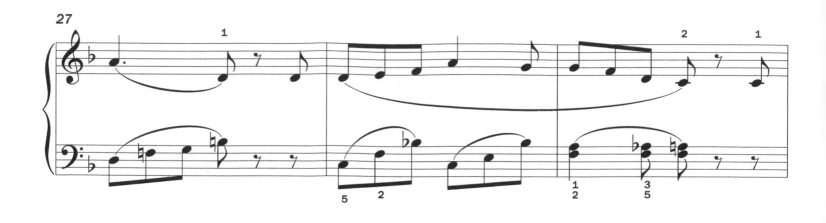

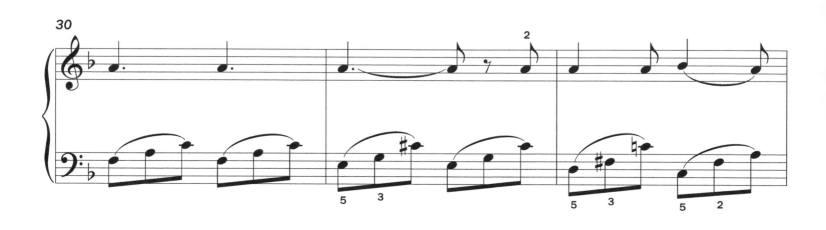

rit.

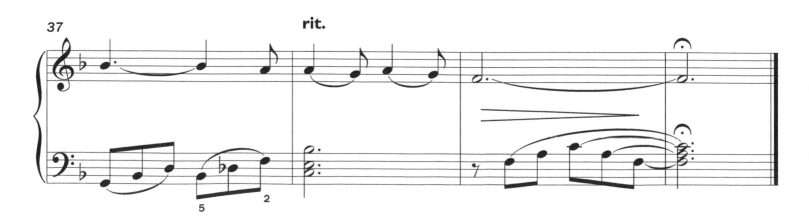

MAD WORLD

Words and Music by
ROLAND ORZABAL

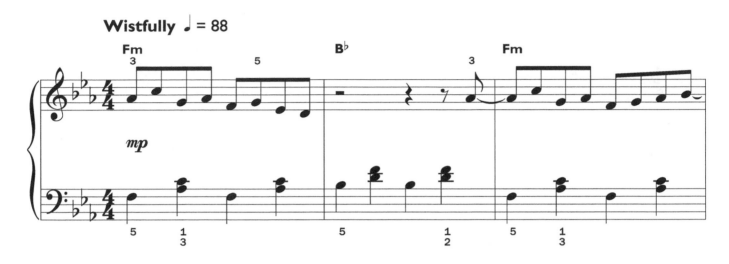

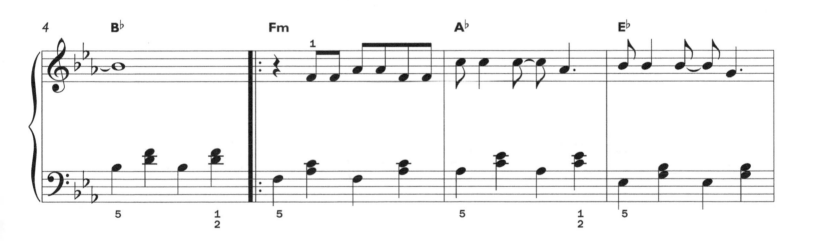

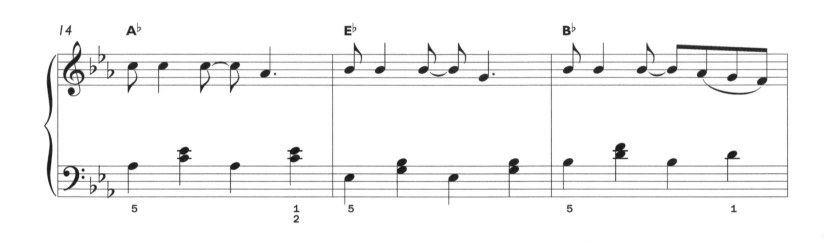

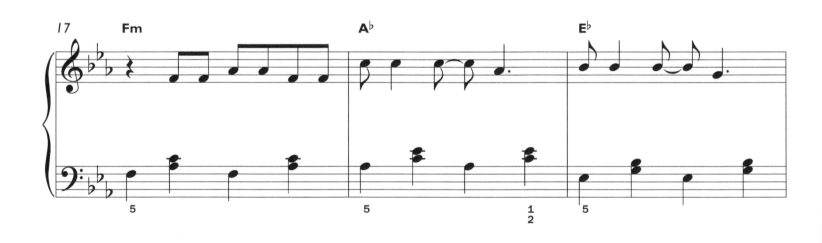

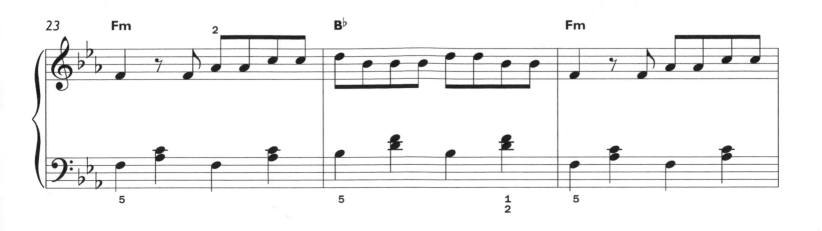

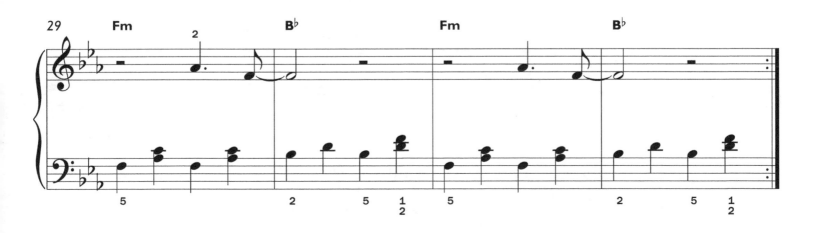

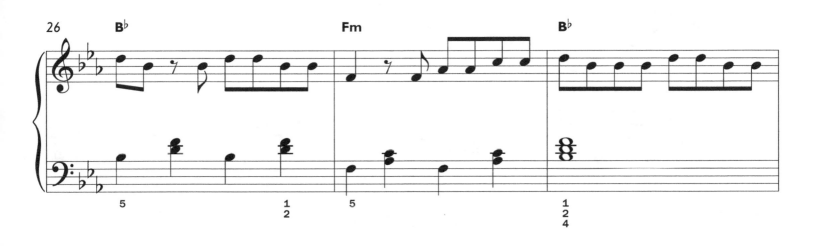

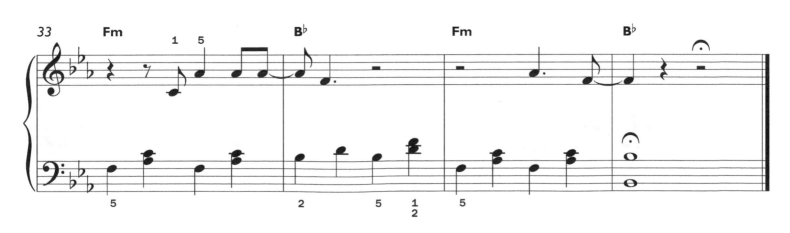

PIANO SONATA NO. 14 IN C# MINOR
("Moonlight") Op. 27 No. 2 First Movement Theme

By LUDWIG VAN BEETHOVEN

Adagio sostenuto

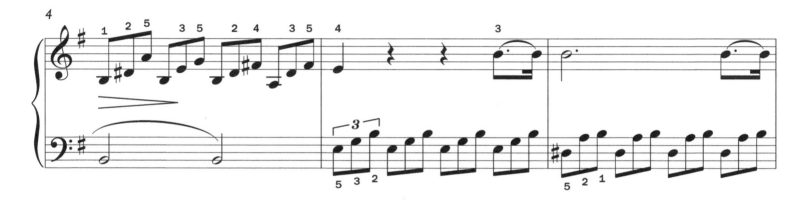

poco rit.   A tempo

THE MUSIC OF THE NIGHT
from THE PHANTOM OF THE OPERA

Music by ANDREW LLOYD WEBBER
Lyrics by CHARLES HART
Additional Lyrics by RICHARD STILGOE

Andante, with expression

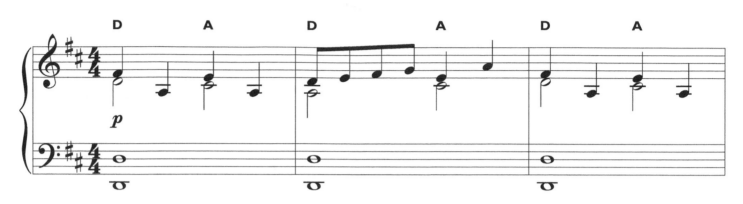

PAVANE POUR UNE INFANTE DEFUNTE

By MAURICE RAVEL

Steadily, with expression ♩ = c.60

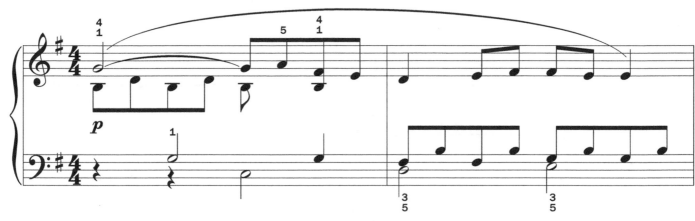

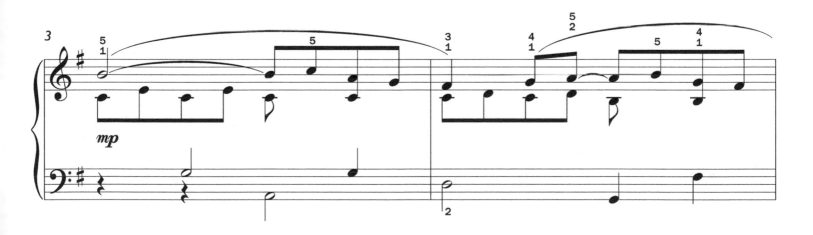

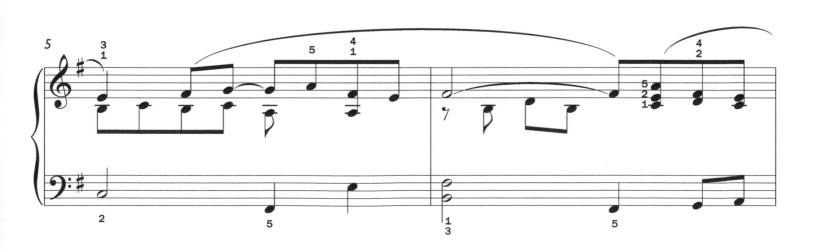

To Coda ⊕

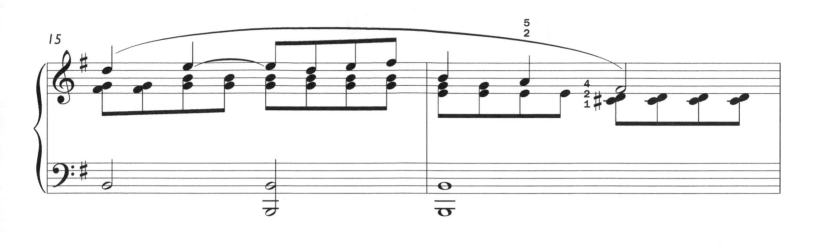

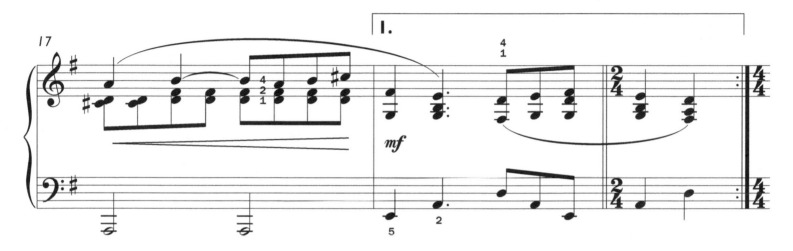

1.

2.

D.C. al Coda

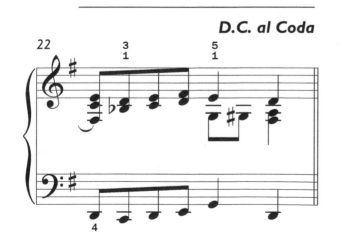

Coda

NOCTURNE IN E FLAT MAJOR OP.9 NO.2

By FREDERIC CHOPIN

Andante

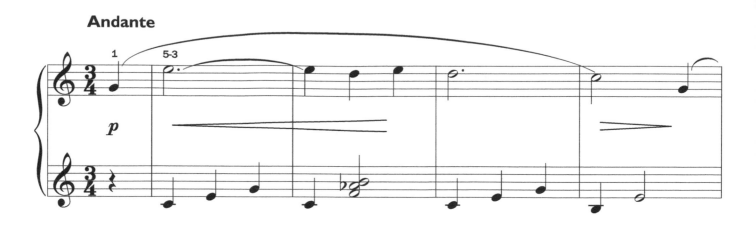

rit.   A tempo

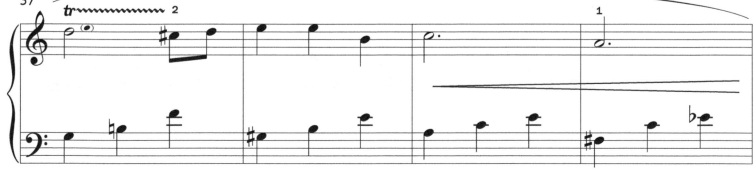

rit.

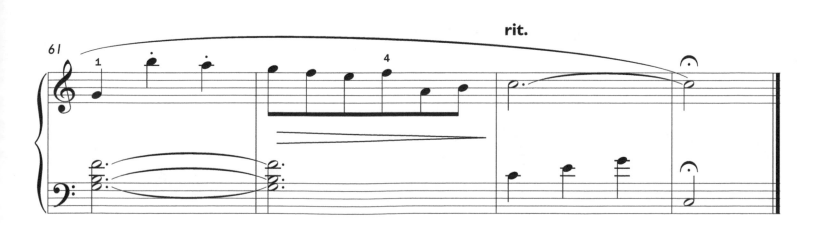

ON MY OWN
from LES MISERABLES

Music by CLAUDE-MICHEL SCHÖNBERG
Lyrics by ALAIN BOUBLIL, JEAN-MARC NATEL,
HERBERT KRETZMER, JOHN CAIRD
and TREVOR NUNN

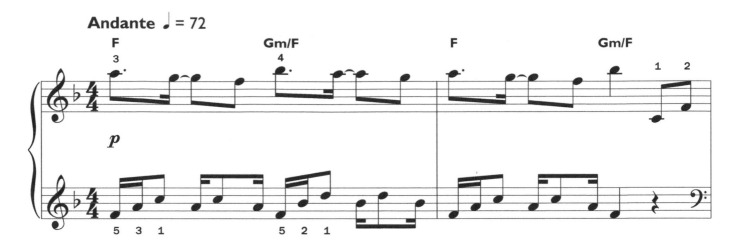

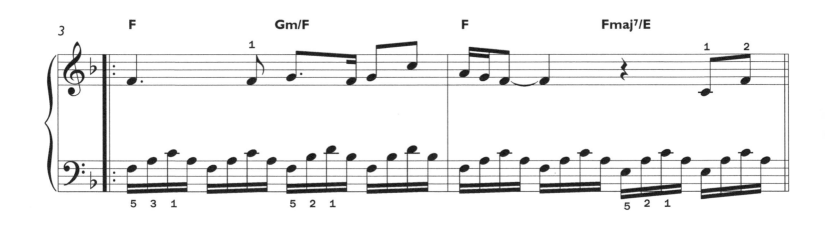

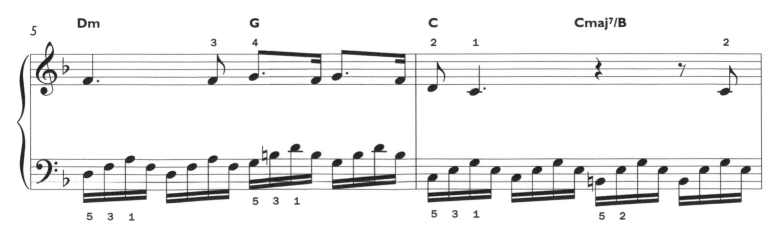

109

POLITIK

Words and Music by GUY BERRYMAN,
JON BUCKLAND, WILL CHAMPION
and CHRIS MARTIN

111

PRELUDE IN C MAJOR
from THE WELL-TEMPERED CLAVIER, BOOK 1

By JOHANN SEBASTIAN BACH

Moderato

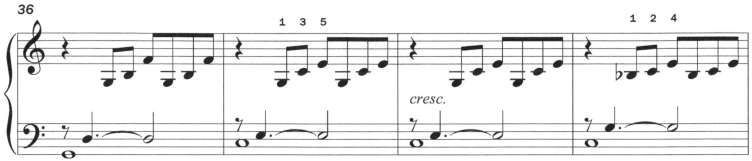

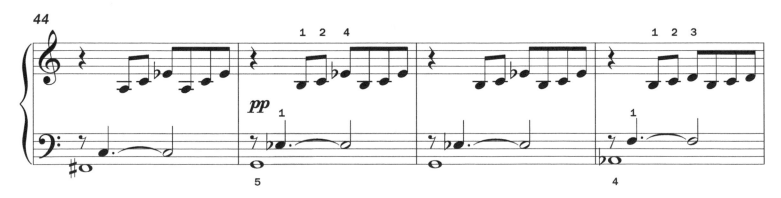

poco rit.

TRÄUMEREI

By ROBERT SCHUMANN

WALTZ FOR DEBBY

Lyric by GENE LEES
Music by BILL EVANS

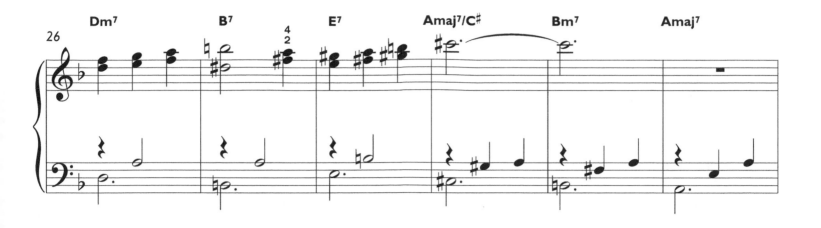

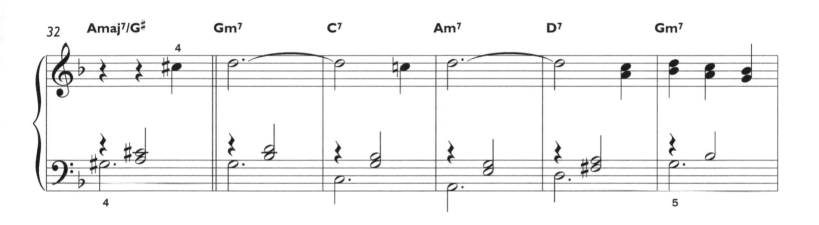

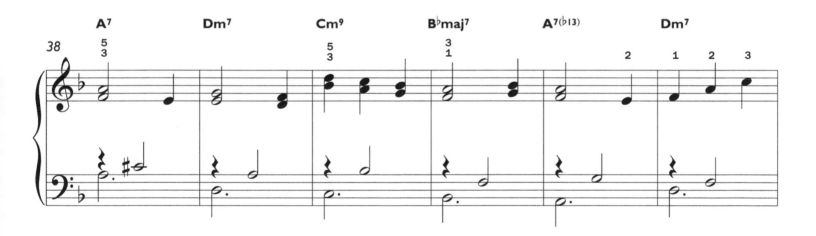

D.C. al Coda

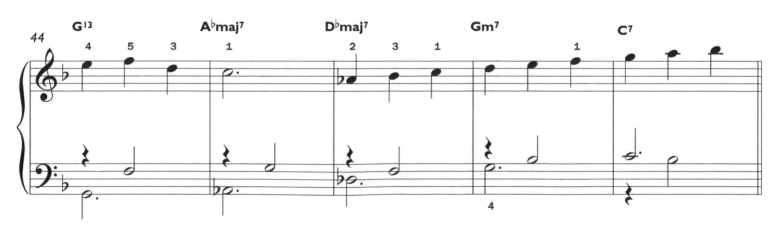

Coda

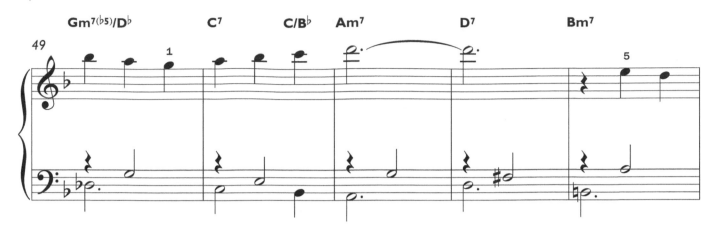

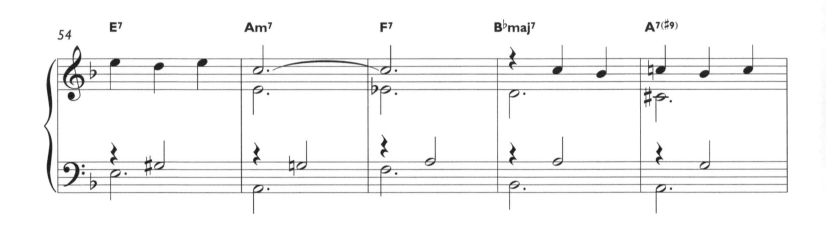

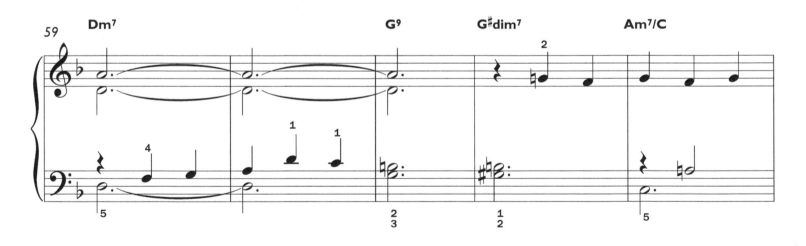

rit. poco a poco

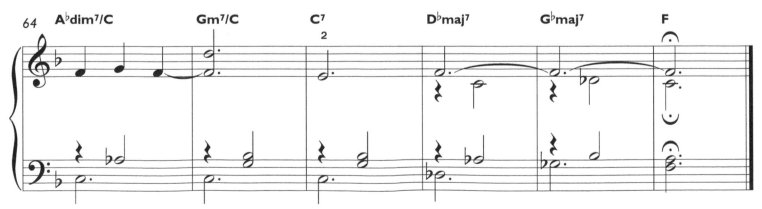

WITHOUT YOU

Written by PETER HAM
and TOM EVANS

Tenderly and slowly ♩ = 63

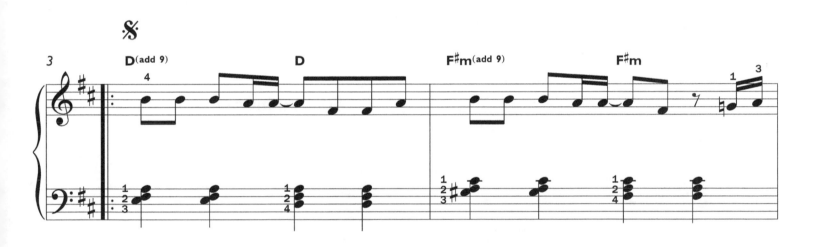

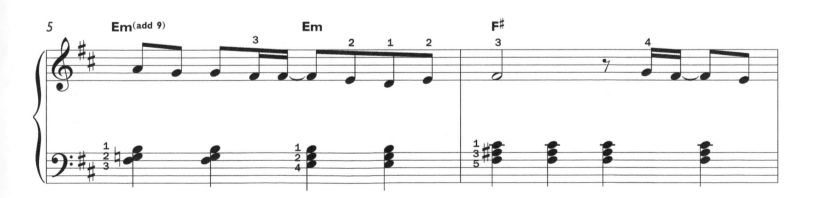

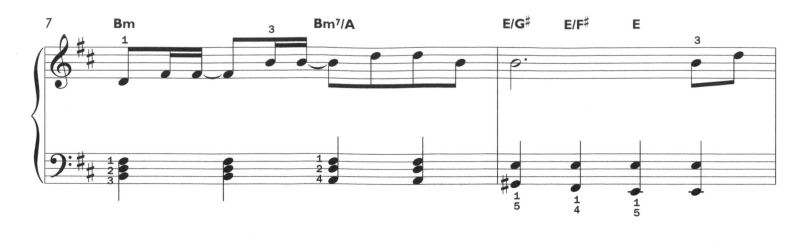

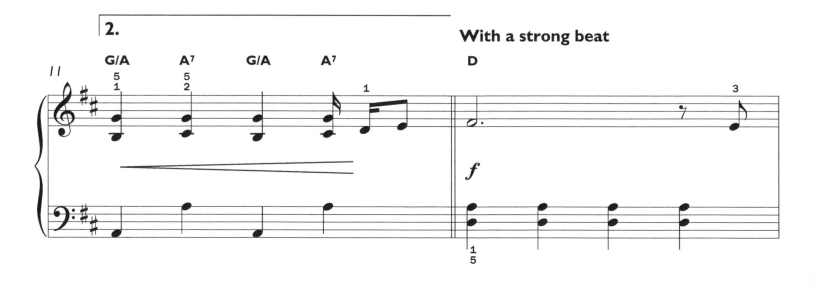

With a strong beat

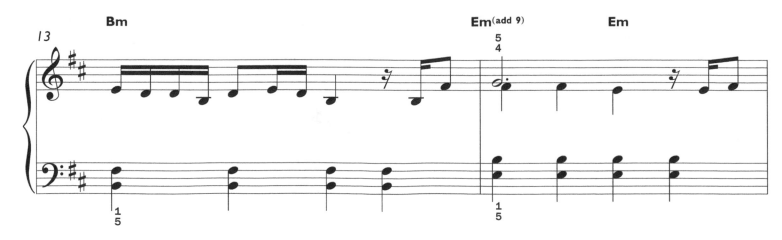

YESTERDAY

Words and Music by JOHN LENNON
and PAUL McCARTNEY

Moderately, with expression

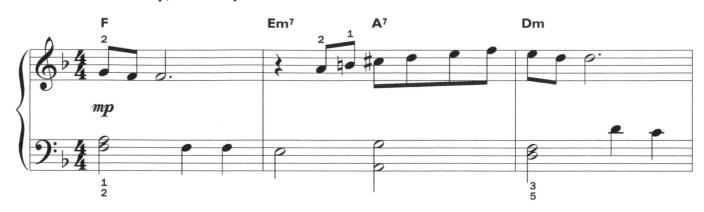

YOUR SONG

Words and Music by ELTON JOHN
and BERNIE TAUPIN

Slow, but pushing forward ♩ = 60

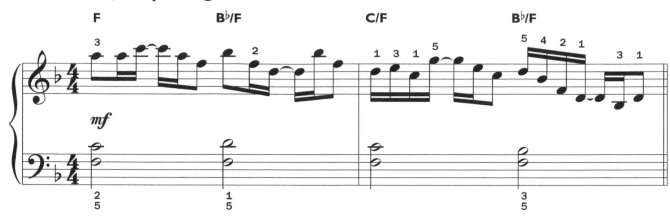

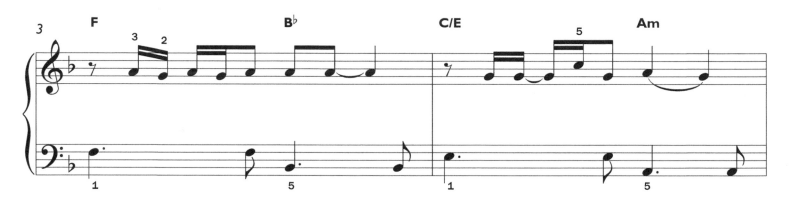

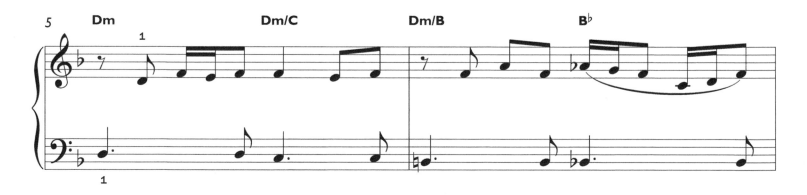

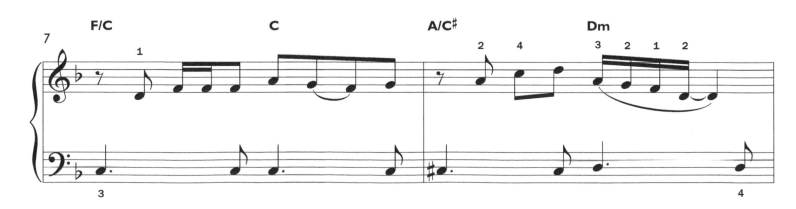